THE HUNT

THE TRUE STORY OF ALASKA'S MOST NOTORIOUS SERIAL KILLER, ROBERT HANSEN

RYAN GREEN

For Helen, Harvey, Frankie and Dougie

Disclaimer

This book is about real people committing real crimes. The story has been constructed by facts but some of the scenes, dialogue and characters have been fictionalised.

Polite Note to the Reader

This book is written in British English except where fidelity to other languages or accents are appropriate. Some words and phrases may differ from US English.

YOUR FREE BOOK IS WAITING

CONTENTS

Wicked Game

Her face felt cold. Wet. Not unfamiliar, given her line of work, but this, this was different. It was a sharp cold, cutting, sending jagged little shots into her head, into her bones. She felt groggy, not like a couple of beers and a couple of smokes groggy but more like 'Did you get the number of the truck that hit me?' groggy. There was a weird metallic taste in her mouth. Weird tastes, also part of the job, but this wasn't the usual salty bitterness. It was blood. Why could she taste blood? What the hell happened last night?

There was really only one way to tell. She had to open her eyes. Or at least the one that wasn't pressed up against the wet, cold whatever it was she was lying on.

She didn't open them. Not yet. First, she listened.

You didn't survive in this bitch of a world by being careless. If there was somebody nearby, somebody watching and waiting for her to stir so that whatever the hell happened last night could happen again even harder, then she didn't want to tip them off that she knew what was going on around her until the last possible second.

So, she lay very still and kept on breathing as smoothly as she could, and she listened. There was a dripping sound, water falling onto something soft. That went with whatever was making her face wet. Snow, obviously snow. She could feel the almost electric tingles as she exhaled and the tiny flakes drifted up to melt on her face. Snow meant outside. Outside meant witnesses. She was already safer than she'd thought.

Outside also meant that it was possible, if not likely, that nothing too horrible had happened last night. Maybe she just got into a fight or had too much to drink. Maybe the sinister whisper in the back of her head telling her that she was really screwed was wrong. It wouldn't be the first time she'd been wrong about something. Not the first time that she'd let her better judgement get clouded and convinced herself that a situation was worse than it was. No actually, it would be the first time. Usually, if she was misjudging, it was in the other direction and she ended up with stitches, a jail sentence, or a loan taken out in her name by some dude that she could barely even remember. Underestimating the danger had always been her problem, so she reminded herself not to do it this time. She would keep her eyes shut, breathe steady, and listen.

Drip drop of melting snow, pattering down all around. Not in town then, where it would all be running along lines around her, but somewhere outside where the forests still grew thick and dense. She had to suppress a shudder. Not from the cold, but from the realisation. There were bears out here. Wolves too. This was Alaska, and if you went for a happy little hike in these woods, you took a rifle with you or you didn't come back. And here she was in her going-out-for-the-night clothes, not even a proper jacket or scarf. She was beyond screwed, even if there was nothing bad going on. And there was definitely something bad going on because otherwise, she'd be able to remember how the hell she got here.

Her head throbbed. The cold of the snow had actually been helping to numb it before, but now that she was paying attention, it didn't feel like a hangover or a fistfight. It felt like somebody had clubbed her over the back of the head. Oh goddamnit, had some stupid construction worker donkey-punched her, thought she was dead, and dumped her out here? If he had, she wouldn't have been paid. She'd have to track the prick, and shake him down, then threaten to go to the cops. What a pain in the ass.

Still, she didn't move. If it was some jackass pulling the old donkey punch and he was still out there, he might not take kindly to her waking up again. People were funny like that. They got themselves all worked up and convinced that the only way out was to keep on killing once they thought they'd done it before. If she suddenly wasn't dead, that didn't mean he'd pull his head out of his ass long enough to realise that she wasn't exactly in a position to be pressing charges.

So, whether it was a donkey punch, a bar fight, or whatever it was that left her out here in the snow with blood in her mouth and an ache in her head like someone had taken to her with a two-by-four, all that mattered now was surviving the next five minutes. Just five minutes. Anyone could survive five minutes. People survived five minutes all day, every day.

She kept her eyes shut, and her ears open. There was nobody else out here. If there was, she'd hear them moving around in the snow. If they weren't moving around, she'd hear them breathing. No question. It was dead silence out in the woods, nothing but the patter of water and the creak of the wood. If somebody was out here, she'd know it.

Even so, she went on playing possum. If she was right about there being nobody around, then she'd spend an extra few minutes lying in the snow that she didn't need to. But if she was wrong, wasting a few more minutes lying still was the least of her worries.

Listening as hard as she could with her head still throbbing, she searched for any tiny hint as to where she might be, and what might be going on. Those damned drips just kept on going, distracting her every time that she thought she might have been hearing something else. Cars going by, the seaplanes coming down, anything that could help her pinpoint where the hell she was. Then just as she was losing her cool, she heard it, soft as a whisper. The running of a river gurgling along, swollen with the snowmelt.

Where the hell was there a river near town?

She knew her way around Anchorage pretty well for somebody who hadn't grown up there. She knew all the alleyways that got quiet in the early morning hours where you wouldn't have to run the risk of a run-in with the motel owners. She knew all the little shortcuts that could take her from one side of town to the other in a hurry if somebody was looking for her that she didn't think ought to be.

But at the edge of town, her geographical knowledge took a nosedive. She didn't go out there. Nobody with any sense went out there. Beyond the cold comforts of town, this place was like the Wild West and the third circle of hell all mixed up together, so cold your eyes could freeze shut and you wouldn't even be able to see the grizzly monster creeping up on you. Law and order ended with the tarmac. In the woods, the law of the wild reigned supreme. Kill or be killed.

Well not really, there were plenty of folks who came out here to hunt or for work. Some even came for fun if they were crazy enough, and most of them made it home with a tall tale of some Mexican stand-off between them and the wildlife or Mother Nature herself. Then there were the wannabe tough guys – they accounted for most of her clientele. They'd tell her all about how brave they had to be just to stroll out to the pipeline and clock in for their day. From her experience, the real tough guys didn't need to brag and didn't feel the need to impress anybody. They were the ones that you had to keep a proper eye on if you wanted to make it out alive. The quiet ones.

Some spark of recognition stirred in her. Last night there had been a quiet one. Not one of the rough and ready survivalist types that she usually saw. A normal-looking guy, like you might find in any other state. He'd been quiet, yeah, but she'd figured he was just bashful. Not used to spending his hard-earned cash on a hot, tight body. He'd get used to it though, they all did. They all came back for more after the first time – she gave them a night to remember.

But she still couldn't remember what had happened afterwards. There had been a titty bar with strippers up on the stage and her Mr Bashful propping up against the bar, hardly even looking their way. Given the lack of interest he was so deliberately showing to the girls who were up there shimmying for their lives, she wondered if he was brought up righteous or if he was queer. Usually, she wouldn't have even bothered approaching a guy like that. Better to wait until all the dancers had gotten him worked up and willing to part from cash, and then swoop in. That was the smart play when you were looking for work in a place like that.

But there had been something about him, something about the set of his shoulders or the bolt-uprightness of his back, that told her a different story from what he was trying to tell. He might have been playing it ice-cool, but that didn't mean he wasn't all wound up inside. She'd have guessed that a guy like that, who couldn't even let it show when a girl had him hot and pent up, was liable to go off like a volcano at the slightest provocation. That'd make her life a lot easier. The sooner he popped, the sooner she could move on to the next guy.

She'd slung herself onto the stool beside him and given him the patented batting of the eyelashes and in short order, the transaction was made. Cash passed hand to hand, in advance, with no resistance, to her absolute surprise. They'd headed out from the gentleman's club to find somewhere for her to pay off her side of the deal and...that's when everything got dark and fuzzy in her memory.

He had been a nice guy, a normal guy, not one of those animals in a man's skin that they had out working the pipeline. He'd been a local, a townie, a normal guy. What the hell could have gone so wrong with Bashful that she'd ended up out here next to a river she'd never even known existed?

She wasn't getting any younger, and she wasn't getting any safer. The longer she was out here, the worse the odds of her making it. For all she knew wolves were already on her scent. She needed to get back to town, fast.

Besides, what was life without taking a few risks? She opened her eyes. At first, it was just a quick flicker before she shut them again quick. The encroaching snow stung at them. The light made fireworks go off inside her head and made her taste blood all over again. Made her want to puke up her guts and curl in a ball and just let the wolves have her. But she couldn't. She couldn't give up, not now, not ever. All her life had been hardship, and she had struggled through it. Every day from now to the grave was going to be a hardship, and she'd go on struggling through it. Because that was what surviving was, looking at all the stuff that wanted you to stop and keeping on going all the same.

Bracing herself for the pain, she opened her eyes again, and forced them to stay open, even as she made the agonising roll away from the snowbank that her face had been propped up on. The land was a black and white negative of trees and snow. Flashing by so quickly that it made her stomach turn over.

There was another ache now. One down between her legs. All the rest might have been new and scary, but that was an old one. One she'd known since she was old enough to bleed. Someone had been with her last night, inside her last night, while she was unconscious. It might have been before the lights went out and she'd lost the memory, but judging by the weight of the ache and the bruises she could feel on her thighs now that she concentrated, it had been after. When she'd been too insensible to stop him, too powerless to push him off when he jackhammered her too hard and left her in agony. It had simmered down now that she'd stopped moving, just a white-hot coal trapped between the crux of her thighs instead of anything blazing brighter. But it would be back. She'd been here enough times to know, it would be back, and it would be worse. Her stomach turning over, and recriminations bleeding through her thoughts, blaming herself for being a victim again, for being so stupid as to trust a man just because he didn't look like a monster. She had known since she was a little girl that the monsters were real, and they looked just like everybody else, why had she gone on trying to convince herself otherwise all these years?

Now wasn't the time to get lost in her own thoughts. Now wasn't the time to feel sorry for herself. She had to get up. She had to move. It might have been mid-morning now, but the sun set fast up here in the north. If she had too far to go back to town, she might not make it, and she did not want to spend another night out in these woods. Only luck could have kept her alive this long, and she'd known with blood slick down her thighs just how good her luck was in the long run.

She could see her breath. Looking down, she could see her skirt had been hiked right up sometime through the night, leaving the pale tops of her thighs exposed, and what she'd been wearing underneath was long gone, but the cold was almost a relief compared to the burning, so she was in no hurry to fix it. Up top, she was dressed like she was going to a bar, not the winter woods. Something light and strappy, meant to show off the goods, not stop the goods from frosting over. Whichever way the town was, she needed to get there fast. She was probably already sick after god knows how long lying in the snow before she came back to consciousness, but another few hours at these temperatures and she was going to start shutting down. Forget staying out here another night, if the sun went down she was going to stop, drop, and frost up. A corpse, pre-frozen for the morgue.

Pushing herself up onto her elbows didn't work so great, there still didn't seem to be any strength in her limbs. She didn't know whether that was because of the head injury that she assumed was responsible for the unconsciousness, the taste of blood, the lost time, and all the rest, or if it was due to the amount of time she had been left lying out in the bitter cold. Either way, she found her arms were not of much use in helping her up. Setting the heel of her boot into the ground, she pushed. It drove her up against the snowbank, but the penalty for that slight movement of her lower half was a new searing pain that shot from her crotch all the way up to her diaphragm. Despite the agonizing pain, she set her other foot down and pushed, driving herself upward against the solid edge of the snowbank.

It took longer than she would have liked to admit to get herself into a sitting position. It scared her how much effort it had taken, how much energy it had cost. It made her wonder if she could make it back to civilization, even if she did know the way. How bad had she been hit?

She touched her hand tentatively to her nose, then to her ears. It came away without blood, but that might have just been because it was frozen, not because it wasn't there. With the same cautious probing fingers, she reached up to touch her scalp. Sharp pain immediately shot across it. She wasn't even close to the central point of impact where the pain was flaring like somebody had dropped a nuke on her skull, but just touching anywhere on her head was enough to make her guts churn.

There was nothing like a good head injury to make your day interesting.

Her neck ached too, of course, the way that necks always do when you hurt your head bad enough. It felt like the pain was radiating down her neck to her shoulders, pulling the muscles tighter and tighter. Normally she'd put her head back, rest it on the snow, take the weight off her neck, but she knew if her head touched anything right now, she would probably start screaming and never stop.

"Alright... Just sit for a minute." She breathed it in, the sharp harsh winter waking her up, making her lungs ache. "Work out the way to town. Go."

Her words sounded thick in her mouth, slurred. Maybe the last remnants of sleep clinging to her tongue, maybe the head wound was even worse than it felt. Maybe it was one of those, life-is-never-the-same kind of head wounds that you heard about sometimes from the loggers. When a guy comes back to town having left who he really was somewhere out in the woods, never to be seen again.

There was no landmark that she recognised out here in the woods, no hint which way town might be. If only she'd stuck it out with Girl Guides, maybe she'd know which way to go. Wasn't there something about moss growing on only one side of a tree? Something about always turning right? Was it "when you're lost always walk downhill?" She couldn't remember. Smoking and boys and disco music had always sounded much more appealing than learning to tie knots.

She was still alive, though. That was the important thing. All the other stuff could come later. As long as she was still alive, she could get herself out of this. It didn't matter if it was going to be hard, or if she was going to have to struggle and hurt. She would make it, and she would survive. Same as she always had.

All she had to do was think. That's all. Just think. It didn't matter if her head hurt. It didn't matter if the white snow and black-striped shadows of the trees kept blending together into a grey blur before sharpening up again. All that mattered was that she was still here, and she could get herself out of this like she had a million other times with a million other problems. She was a survivor.

"River... river's over there." She dragged her head around towards the source of the distant sound mumbling to herself. "Follow... the river... to the sea. That's... that's how you do it, right?"

Anchorage was on the sea, in the Cook Inlet, reaching out a sleepy hand towards Fire Island. If she found a river, it would lead her to something. Even if she couldn't find town, she didn't think there was a single river anywhere near the town that didn't have one fisherman or another out on their boat all day chasing down sockeye salmon. Some of them even had cabins out here.

Them and the hunters were serious about it. Maybe she didn't even need to find the town, just one of those cabins. Someplace to get warmed up, get herself together. Someplace she could wait for help to come. She wanted to see a doctor about her head as soon as she could, but if it came to it, she wasn't above hunkering down until help arrived. She wasn't proud. Whatever it took to survive, right?

Drawing in ragged breaths, she shifted until her palms were pressing down into the bitter-sharp snow. One big push, then she'd be up to her feet. There were trees all around, if she felt dizzy, she could just grab onto one of them.

All it would take was one big push. Just... push. Her hands shook, vibrations running up to her elbows as she strained, she tried to get her feet beneath her, but they slipped away in the powdery snow. Growling with frustration, she twisted around, tucking up her knees, getting them underneath her and getting up that way.

Then she heard motion.

All this time as she'd struggled and wriggled and wrestled her way to sitting upright, he'd just been watching her, completely silent, completely still. Not like a person sitting still, but like a rock, a bit of furniture, something so immobile that you don't even notice it until you stub your toe. He might have been one of the trees for all that she'd noticed him.

He'd stayed all but invisible until now, impossible to perceive because of his incredible stillness. She couldn't believe that in the forest silence, she hadn't even heard his breath. Hadn't seen a puff of it drifting by. It was like he was a dead man.

The noise she'd heard, she had no doubt she'd only heard because he wanted her to hear it. The tell-tale click-clack of a rifle loading.

He stood before her now, looking all too normal for such a strange place in his big jacket, his fur hat, rifle strap dangling all casual-like off the rifle he held in his hands. Not pointed at her, just there. She didn't recognise him at first. His was just one of those faces that you saw around town sometimes. Blending into the background. He'd always been there, and he always would be, and she'd never give him a second glance. Nobody would. But here he was, standing out for the first time. Standing out in the middle of the silent forest with a gun in his hand. Her only hope of survival.

Relief should have hit then. Relief that she wasn't alone in this bleak winter wonderland. Relief that there was somebody out there who could take her home. Who could keep her safe.

Relief didn't come. Nothing about this guy felt safe. Not here, outside the context of town. Not after that shit he'd just pulled, pretending he wasn't there when she was obviously in desperate need of help. She looked up at his face now, shadowed by his hat, features blurring and swirling as her eyes slipped in and out of focus. She couldn't make him out, not completely, not yet. She reached out a hand to him, not so subtly begging for help to stand, but he remained completely immobile and implacable, like a glacier.

With a strength that she didn't know she had in her, she got her feet tucked under herself and pushed her way up to standing. The whole world spun around, twirling and swirling like when she was a kid on a carousel back down south. Back when she could convince herself that there was somebody that loved her and her days weren't filled with this awful biting cold. Warmth. God, she missed warmth.

When the world stopped turning and her eyes were able to focus, she looked at him again, searching for any hint of mercy or humanity in his features.

It had taken her this long to recognise him, not because of blurry eyes or deep shadows or the hat, but because without any light behind his eyes, he looked like a completely different person. There was no expression on his face, no sympathy, no lust, nothing she could work with at all. He was a solid stone wall that she'd never be able to break through or climb over. But she knew him. Slowly, like he had all the time in the world, he lifted his hand from his rifle and pointed past her.

"That's the Knik River." Bashful told her, no longer bashful, no longer anything at all but pure cold stitched into human skin. "We're northeast of town a few miles. You want to be heading away from it, not towards it if you're going to get back there before sunset."

She'd never been this far out before, but the Knik, that was easy enough to fit into the map in her head. There were two arms of the Cook Inlet giving Anchorage a big hug, one of them was the Knik Arm, fed into by the Knik River, she guessed. How far up did the arm become the river? How far out had he taken her?

It now felt obvious to her that he didn't mean for her to walk away from this alive. You don't take a whore out into the middle of the unexplored wilderness so you can have a nice quiet chat with them, and you don't take them out so that they can perform for you. There was no good reason to be isolated from everyone and everything unless he meant to hurt her. To kill her. She knew that with a certainty that shocked her. Not because she lacked an imagination of all the other reasons a man might want this sort of privacy, or because she hadn't experienced some of the weird and wild things that men liked, but because of him. Bashful wasn't human. Not anymore. The mask of humanity had slipped away from him along with his stutter. Every word he spoke came out as crisp and clear as the winter air.

She had so many questions tickling at her throat. What are you? Why are you like this? Why are you doing this to me? What's the point of bringing me out here? Why? Why? Why?

She settled on the practical question that might help. "Why are you telling me this?"

There was a movement then, the tiniest hint of a nod. Like she was an animal that had been taught to do a trick and had performed it to her master's satisfaction. No point smiling at a dog or giving it a round of applause, it wouldn't understand anyway, but all the same, she felt like she'd done something right. Like she'd won a point in whatever game he was playing by asking the right thing at the right time.

His hand moved back to the rifle, but otherwise, she could have sworn not a single hair on his head had budged, it was like he was a still picture pasted into a movie. It was beyond uncanny. And it was making her nervous in a way she couldn't quite describe. She supposed this was how a mouse felt when a cat was watching it, but it wasn't able to see the cat that was about to hurt it.

"It makes things fair. If you get away but you go the wrong way, you'd die out there all the same. Now, if you make it. You're free."

From the moment she'd seen him, she had her suspicions about how this was going to go. She'd expected threats, a demand for a performance, maybe a few minutes that she'd prefer not to remember later which bourbon might help with, but not this. What was the point? He already had her. He had her so completely in his power that she didn't even pretend that any part of her life was still hers. To survive when somebody had you like that, you had to submit. It might have gone against her every instinct to simply roll over and let some man tell her what she had to do, but it was how you survived. The only sure way to survive an encounter like this. Say what they wanted you to say, do what they wanted you to do, then go away somewhere inside your mind so that it was happening to somebody else. That was how you survived it. That was how you came out the other side still whole.

What he was saying made no sense. If he'd wanted her dead, she would already be dead. He had had plenty of opportunity. He'd clearly taken advantage of some of those opportunities. Her crotch wouldn't feel like somebody had jammed a hot poker in it otherwise. But when he had the opportunity to kill her in her sleep while she was completely defenceless and to eliminate any possibility of her saying anything to anyone, he had chosen to wait and allow her to wake up. It made no sense for him to kill her now. Hurt her, maybe, rape her again, probably, but kill her? It just didn't make sense. "What do you mean, if I make it?"

There was no nod this time. No 'good girl' and a pat on the head. He wasn't pleased by that question. He looked at her like she'd failed to sit on command. Then, as if he was explaining one and one making two to a toddler, he explained everything, everything that would define what the rest of her life was going to be. Everything that he was. Everything. It took only three little words, and she couldn't quite comprehend them.

"I'm a hunter."

She stared at him. He was dressed like he was going out hunting in the woods, just like nearly every man in Anchorage dressed to go out and try to bag an elk to fill their freezer for the winter. It was obvious that he was a hunter. They were all hunters up here. They had to be, with food costing what it did to ship up from the lower forty-eight. If they didn't hunt, there just wouldn't be enough food to go around. Fortunately, the great big Alaskan wilderness offered more food hoofing about than everyone in town could consume in a hundred lifetimes.

But that wasn't what he was saying. She wanted to pretend it was what he was saying. Pretend it wasn't real. That none of this was real. That it was all just some misunderstanding that they could both walk away from intact. She didn't want to believe that he could mean that he wanted... She didn't want to believe that anyone could want that. That anyone could be so sick and twisted that they could look at another person and consider them to be prey. "You can't be serious."

His face told her everything else that she needed to know. Everything that the three words had meant.

This wasn't a joke, this wasn't a misunderstanding, this was real. She was a survivor, and you didn't survive by pretending the world wasn't the way it was. That men weren't the way that they were, even though it might sicken you to know the truth of it.

She'd known men before where the sex came second to the pain. Men who'd wanted her pain more than anything else in the world, no matter what it cost them. Nor did it matter what it cost her to go along with it, to act like it was all for fun when she knew that she'd be the one covered in bruises, bleeding and sobbing, curled up on the floor of her shower, praying that when she looked in the mirror there wouldn't be anything for anyone else to see. For anyone else to judge.

"Ten."

His voice startled her into motion. She took one staggering step away, primal instinct screaming at her to run, but she had to try and get out of this. The dude was holding a hunting rifle like he knew how to use it, and forest or not, she didn't like her chances.

"You're kidding me." She gave voice to her confusion, even though she knew she shouldn't, and it earned her another blank expression. Disapproving. Playing the game wrong.

He hadn't moved a muscle. Hadn't brought the gun up to take aim. Hadn't even changed his expression. He was completely still, but it was different now. Not like a rock, more like a tiger, coiled and ready to pounce. Now when he spoke to her, his eyes weren't staring off into the woods as if he was pretending that he was the only person out here. They were locked onto her. Tracking her movement. Calculations about wind speed and direction ticking away behind the expression that gave nothing away, not even his excitement.

"Nine."

She did the unthinkable, she found the courage to step forward, even as her body screamed at her to run and keep on running. To hide and cower. To do anything, anything, so that she wasn't here. Wasn't facing what she now knew with an awful certainty was coming. "Come on man, I won't say nothing to nobody, just take me home. We can forget all about..."

He cut her off. "Eight."

There was no reasoning with him. No logic that might dissuade him. No humanity to appeal to. She might as well have been talking to one of the bears or the wolves she knew were out here. At least they might have reacted, might have cocked their head to the side and acknowledged that there was a sound being made. This guy didn't even give her that. He just watched her like she was some germ under a microscope, and he waited.

"Seven."

She took off running. There was nothing else left to do. No hope of getting out of this alive, except for doing exactly what he wanted. Probably not even then. She didn't know how far up north the Knik River was. Didn't know how many miles of wilderness lay between her and the promised freedom. She had never bothered to learn, never planning to come out here, unless somebody paid the overnight rate to keep their hunting cabin warm for them, and even then, she'd have thought twice about it. It was too dangerous, too isolated, anything could happen out here and nobody would ever find out about it.

Anything *was* happening out here, and nobody would ever find out about it. Would they even find her body? Would there be a funeral? Would anyone even notice that she had gone missing, or would they just think that she'd moved along like so many other women did when they got tired of the cold and the dark and the rough hands of working men who didn't know how to treat a girl right?

"Six."

She could still hear him, counting down, she hadn't made it far enough between "seven" and "six" to be out of hearing range which meant that as she scrambled through the fallen branches and undergrowth, he could hear her too. Even if she managed to get out of sight, even if she managed to duck down some gully or hide behind a copse of trees thick enough to keep her hidden, he'd still be able to track her by sound.

"Five."

His voice was distant now. Further off than she could have hoped that it might be. Maybe by the next number, she wouldn't hear him at all. He'd given her too much of a head start. She was going to make it. Those ten counts would get her so far away that he'd never have a chance of catching her all the way out here. There was so much empty country to cover. She broke right, sprinting off at an angle to the direction of town, she could right her heading later, but right now she needed to focus on losing him. Once she knew she was safe, she'd be able to hike back to town at her leisure. Well, not at her leisure, because she'd still be slowly succumbing to hypothermia and frostbite and all the other terrible stuff that happened to you if you went roaming around in your bar clothes in the middle of the forest in the middle of Alaskan winter.

"Four."

She couldn't hear him saying it, but she could hear his voice, cold and clipped, in her head. If she made it out of this alive, she was willing to bet that she'd be hearing a lot of that voice. Every time she laid down to try and get some sleep, she'd hear him counting down to her death. Every moment that she thought she was at peace, he'd be there.

"Three."

She slipped as she was heading down an embankment, in such a rush that her legs just went on windmilling as she fell. The impact knocked the wind out of her lungs and sent the pain in her head, pain that she'd almost forgotten about, back into overdrive. She had to bite back a scream or risk giving away her location. She would have lost everything because of a stupid slip and fall. She could taste blood in her mouth again. She'd bitten her lip to stop herself from crying out. And now she had to get up again, the whole awful arduous experience of pulling herself to her feet played out at double speed, the pain, the nausea and the encroaching darkness all coming in quick succession. She was not going to die out here. She was a survivor. She got up. She turned to glance back the way she'd come, a luxury she hadn't dared allow herself before, as she ran for her life.

"Two."

Stretching out behind her, up the slope and off through the woods were footprints. More than footprints, a whole path that she'd cleared through the snow in her frantic sprint. This guy was a hunter, and she had just left him the clearest trail to follow that she could think of. She had to do something. Didn't they say something about wiping your tracks away with a fallen branch or walking backwards to confuse your tracks or... she couldn't remember any of this shit. School was a distant memory, and the only thing that she'd learned since then was just how low she was willing to sink. She'd never even considered that she might someday need to remember any of this stuff.

"One."

Screw it. The damage was done, she still had her few seconds of advantage, and she was going to use every moment left to her. It didn't matter if he could track her, if she just ran fast enough for long enough, he'd never be able to catch up. Her lungs were burning. Years of twenty a day fighting back against the sudden exertions. They said smoking would kill her, but not like this. Never like this.

"Zero."

Her time was up. She turned south and ran. Faster than he could follow. Faster than a bullet.

She made it almost a mile.

Pocahontas

On February 15th 1939, Robert Christian Hansen was born in Estherville, Iowa. His parents were an American woman named Edna Hansen, and a Dutch man named Christian 'Chris' Hansen, who owned a well-known local bakery. Whether there was some sort of culture clash at play, or if Chris was truly as domineering and aggressive as his son would later describe is unclear. What is clear is that, as the eldest child, a great weight of expectation was placed upon Robert's shoulders almost as soon as he was old enough to walk on his own.

When Robert was a mere three years of age his family had packed up and moved out west to California where his father opened the second of the many bakeries that he would operate throughout his life. He had hoped that the change of locale would result in a significant increase in income and afford his family a more comfortable life. As it turned out, business was not much better and everything cost so much more that the family's hopes of improving their situation were soon dashed. Just as Robert was, ever so slightly, beginning to come out of his shell at school, it was announced over dinner one evening that they would be moving yet again. Back to Iowa.

For a moment, it had seemed like a return to a normalcy that Robert had already forgotten, but they would not be returning to the town of his birth and the minuscule social circle that his mother had managed to cobble together for him there. Instead, they would be relocating to Pocahontas, Iowa. A whole new town, a whole new bakery, a whole new set of strangers.

As a result of never socialising as a child outside of the confines of the home, Robert was painfully shy. Almost incapable of speaking to anyone in school, whether they were teachers or other students. He would not have been popular, even if he hadn't shied away from every social interaction as if it were venomous, but as it was, he could not even hope to attain unpopularity. He was so forgettable even the bullies seemed to overlook him.

"Strict" is a word often thrown around when describing the Hansen household, "disciplined" is another. As a baker, his father had to rise early in the morning, long before the rest of the sleepy suburb in which they lived, and he expected exactly the same from his wife and son. While it was still pitch black and cold, they would assemble in the kitchen to eat breakfast together. Breakfast that his wife was expected to make for him each day without fail or error. These early morning starts did nothing to help young Robert with his faltering social life. By the time that most children his age were attending play-dates and parks in the afternoon, he was nearing the point of complete exhaustion. It was a struggle for him to even make it home from school each day before he wanted to crawl into his bed. But once again, the discipline of his father intervened.

The children would eat their meal with the parents at the set time of six pm. Afterwards, they were expected to spend their evening in their father's company so that he did not feel like they were being neglected thanks to his strict work schedule. After dinner, little Robert was typically beginning to fade, exhausted from the full day of normal activities in addition to the many chores he was assigned around the house. A younger sibling had eventually joined the family but the focus, and the weight of responsibilities, remained firmly on Robert.

To begin preparing him for his adult life, and following in his father's footsteps as everyone expected, Robert was brought to the bakery each morning once he was old enough to provide any help at all. He was set to such menial tasks as could be trusted to a preteen. Scrubbing and cleaning the ovens from the inside. Washing down the counters. Mopping the floors. Setting traps for the rats that seemed intent on destroying everything and anything they could sink their teeth into. It was arduous physical labour, especially for a boy who had not yet developed physically to the point of being capable of doing much of it. Exhaustion went from being a thing that crept up on him slowly throughout the day to being his constant miserable companion. He could no longer remember a time that he was not tired, and even when he was allowed to fall into his bed, he seemed to wake again after only a blink, feeling no amelioration of his weariness.

Somewhat inevitably, he began falling asleep in class and falling behind as a natural result. When his father learned of this, his fury knew no bounds. The boy lacked discipline. He lacked drive and ambition. He seemed to have no interest in anything, no passion. These were all things that Chris had in abundance and was intent on instilling in his son by whatever means were necessary. Whether it was by turning their time together in the evenings into a long lecture on the virtues that he was expected to embody, or by rousing him early from his slumber so that he could be thoroughly corrected on all the errors that he had made in his household chores as well as the chores he had performed at the bakery.

The constant stress of his life and the abuse that he suffered at the hands of his father under the guise of discipline had worn away what little self-esteem the boy might have hoped to cultivate, and gone further still, making every attempt at conversation feel like a minefield that he had to carefully navigate to avoid detonating his father's temper. He began to stutter when trying to speak, and when his father disciplined him for it, it did not improve but only worsened. By the time that most boys were starting to form friendships that would last a lifetime, he had not a single friend to his name. The onset of puberty didn't help matters, his blessed shield of invisibility faded away as a prodigious outbreak of acne covered almost his entire face.

From being entirely forgotten about, he now became a figure of ridicule throughout the whole school. Stuttering, simple, spotty Bob the Baker. Always looking like he was half asleep, too scared to even look at girls, let alone talk to them. Probably for the best, as most girls his age professed that it would be their worst nightmare if he tried to ask them out.

It was yet another failure in the eyes of his father. Robert had no friends, no girlfriend, no interests or hobbies in which he excelled. He was growing up to be a nobody, and that was something that his overbearing father could not tolerate. After consulting with co-workers and visitors to the store about how pathetic and unlikable his son was, Chris came to the conclusion that it was his duty to make a man out of the pathetic runt. To make him masculine and strong, worthy of a woman's attention. So, the next time that the opportunity came along, Chris did the unthinkable. He let someone else open up the bakery so that he and his son could rise at five in the morning and load into the back of one of the neighbour's trucks to head out into the woods and spend the day hunting. Chris had been assured that this would make a man out of the boy. Learning to hunt, to kill, it would teach him self-reliance and instil all the other manly virtues that Chris felt that the boy was so sorely lacking.

It felt like a doomed venture from the very beginning. Robert was half the size of the other boisterous teenagers who were along for the ride, completely isolated from them, despite being forced onto the bench seat alongside them. While they joked and jibed with one another, Robert sat in silence, staring out of the window sullenly. Wondering what fresh hell his father had signed him up for now.

Out in the woods, the boy's eyes widened when the gun rack was rolled out and all the rifles that had been brought along came into sight. Unbidden, his hands reached out for them, only to be slapped away by one of the fathers, who was intent on teaching a lesson on firearm safety before any of these wild teens could start taking potshots at each other as a joke. While the other boys messed around, Robert listened to every word intently. Taking it all in. Memorising every detail of every instruction as if there had never been anything in the world so interesting. By the time the other boys were allowed to even pick up a gun, he was already in the midst of oiling his and checking through all of the components for any sign of wear. It looked ridiculous, an oversized toy in a little boy's hands. Yet while the others joked and laughed and messed around, he was sighting through the scope, correcting for the minute inconsistencies in the magnification, tracing the flight of birds and squirrels from tree to tree. His peers were all there to have a good time, but that boy was there to hunt.

Before long the hunting party had divided into the more serious and avid hunters and those who were just along for the ride. While the latter group contained his peers, Robert found himself with the former group. For once, being separated from everyone his own age did not seem like a punishment. Rather, it felt like he was special, and had been chosen because of that to accompany the more experienced hunters who actually intended to make something of their day.

He was as incompetent as any fresh-faced child is when it comes to hunting, but while his peers were dissuaded by their failures and quit, he kept on going, listening and learning. He had what the others lacked, what his father had spent his whole lifetime trying to instill; discipline.

He wouldn't bag a deer on that first outing, but by the end of the day, most of the adults agreed that they'd be happy to have him back the next time they were heading out. It was an open invitation extended to his father too, even though the baker had shown no competence and scared off more than his share of the prey with the way he stomped around through the undergrowth as if he owned the place. It was here that Chris's and Robert's paths would diverge.

Instead of rising in the dreary early hours to follow in his father's footsteps each weekend, Robert now awoke with a spring in his step and something to look forward to. He went out every Saturday with the local hunters, learning and improving his hunting skills, and on those weeknights when his father came home stomping around and demanding his dinner on the table, more often than not, Robert was not there. Instead, he could be found down at the gun range with some of the old hands who were helping him to improve his technique.

It would not take long before the bread that Chris had brought home was accompanied by meat that his son had hunted and harvested with his own two hands. And still, Robert kept on working at it with singular obsession, turning all the energy that had once been devoted to his father's rigorous demands to this new hobby. It was not long before he was coming home from the range with medals for his marksmanship. He began learning how to use the bow at the recommendation of the other hunters who claimed that exclusively using a rifle was going to become boring for him now that he'd become such a fine shot. They were right about the immense improvement in his marksmanship, but they were wrong about Robert getting bored. He would never tire of hunting. Never tire of killing. It was the one bright spark in an otherwise miserable and drab life.

He moved through the forests like a shadow, putting all the hunters he went out with to shame. If he didn't want to be seen, he wouldn't be. If he didn't want to be heard, he had a way of rolling his feet that seemed to silence the crackling of even the driest of leaves. He took what he'd learned from the grown men who were now his peers, and he improved on it.

School was miserable and home was miserable but out in the wild, Robert felt like he was a whole person. He was not just a joke, a punching bag, or a tool to inflate his father's already bloated sense of self-worth. His life finally had a purpose, and that purpose was to hunt.

Throughout his teenage years, a predictable pattern emerged. He would go off to the shooting range, archery classes, or hunting in the woods and enjoy a sense of equilibrium that had been missing from his life before. He could draw everything down into sharp focus, as he had to when taking aim, and it eliminated all the static in his head, allowing him to feel at peace. But the moment that he returned home, or to school, or to any of the myriad other situations that made him so uncomfortable, all that equilibrium and confidence vanished. His stutter came back in full force.

The only difference was that now, he knew that things didn't have to be this way. He knew that there was a better, happier version of himself. He could have, no, he should have been walking around and living as that version every day of the week but between his father and the school, they beat that better version out of him. With no self-esteem, there had been nothing dangerous about little Robert. When he was picked on, mocked, or forced into situations that made him horribly uncomfortable he accepted that it was just his lot in life. Just like he had come to accept the endless exhaustion. But no more. Now he recognized the unfairness of what was being done to him. Now that he had glimpsed just a little bit of life outside of the box that they had been forcing him into, he began to recognise that he had value, even if others didn't see it. That made him furious. Furious with the teachers for turning a blind eye to his abuse, furious at his peers in school for treating him like he was nothing like he was a joke. And most of all, furious at his father who had set him up for failure from the moment he was born. His own father had pre-emptively ruined any chance that he'd had for a normal life by screaming, bullying, and wheedling him until he couldn't even string together a coherent sentence. He was furious that he'd had to live in fear of tripping over his own words and saying something wrong thereby giving his father yet another trifling excuse to punish him. First came the fury, then came the hate.

As he hit his teenage years full swing and romance started to be a subject of interest, his status as a social pariah prevented him from finding any of the normal outlets for all the hormonal energy that was flooding through him. Women didn't just reject him, they were actively repulsed by him. It didn't matter that some of their dads thought he was a good guy, or that he stood to inherit a pretty solid job when he was older, attraction at that age was all about looks and personality, and Robert Hansen had neither. Even if everyone didn't already look at him as an outcast loser, the fact of the matter was that he was physically incapable of carrying on any type of conversation with a woman thanks to his stutter. Girls made him nervous, and when he was nervous, the stutter came out even more than usual. In regular circumstances, he'd matured enough now to gain some mastery over his own body and push through, but the moment that his nerves became a little frazzled, so too did his ability to string together a full sentence, or even to force out a whole word.

When he was younger, the isolation had made him miserable, that much was true, but the struggles he faced now intensified that misery to a much greater degree. Before, socialising had just been one of those things that happened to other people, but now, on some basic level, he actually needed it. It was the first step in the much-vaunted journey to manhood that his father had seemed so obsessed with. He needed to get a girlfriend to prove that he was a man, that he was everything that they had said he wasn't. His lack of success in that arena served as yet another major frustration in his life, another fount of rage to go with so many others.

Leaving school as early as he was legally allowed, he had no real options except to join his father in the bakery and suffer the endless barbs and arrows of Chris's accusations and recriminations. There was not a day that went by that didn't involve Robert having to briefly excuse himself from the workspace so that he could go someplace private and tremble with barely contained fury.

He hated his father, that much was obvious, but despite that hatred, he still wanted the man's approval more than anything else. He wanted to prove to his father that he was a man, regardless of whatever nebulous definition Chris was measuring by that day. Some days Robert came close, thanks to his hunting and marksmanship, but most days, the long dreary days that filled two years of his life after the end of school, Chris's definition involved absolute compliance without complaint or question. Complete servitude and obedience were required, not from any of the other employees at the bakery, only from Robert. When Chris didn't get his son's complete subservience, he browbeat and abused him. When he did get his son's complete subservience, he looked down on Robert as pathetic and subhuman for grovelling in exactly the manner that he demanded. There was no winning so long as Robert went on playing the game. His home life was completely under Chris's control. His work life was completely under Chris's control. Hunting and his time at the range were still at least partially his own, but more and more, his father was encroaching on that free time with ever-increasing demands. This is not to say that Chris was in any way a hypocrite. He put in more hours at the bakery than anyone else, saw to all his chores, and more. He would be what is now called a 'workaholic' but back in the 1950s, he was considered to be the pinnacle of what a man should be. And he expected his son to be just like him.

On the day of his eighteenth birthday, as soon as it was legal for him to do so, Robert Hansen left home. He was not just attempting to escape from the oppressive situation that he was trapped in there, but also from the situation that followed him to work every single day. He moved out of the family house and quit the family business simultaneously. The year was 1957 and

Robert Hansen had just signed up for the United States Army Reserve.

He spent only one year in the army before being discharged. A year that was apparently fairly unremarkable. Yet when he returned from it to Pocahontas, it was with a renewed humanity. He had finally aged out of his acne problem even though his face would be scarred for the rest of his life, and while his stutter persisted, he had become better at keeping his cool, and thus, keeping it under control. He moved back in with his parents after his time in the reserves, but it was only a temporary situation, no matter what his father might have thought. He was quite willing to help out at the bakery, but the discipline of his time in the army combined with his now fairly expansive experience meant that he was no longer reliant on his father for guidance or drive. He rattled through the necessary routines as the work demanded, and never once went crawling to his father seeking any sort of approval that would doubtlessly be rebuffed. He had grown as a person and Chris, having no idea how to handle it, ended up giving the boy the silent treatment more often than not. That did not bother Robert in the least. He had spent his whole childhood with nobody to talk to and received only abusive criticism when anyone bothered to speak to him. Silence was a happy reprieve from his father's usual relentless demands, so he would take it, and take it gladly.

If Chris had expected that his son's little flight of fancy to the army was the end of the boy's attempts to spread his wings, then he was sorely mistaken. Despite so much of his time being taken up working in the bakery, Robert was not idle. He was constantly seeking out new opportunities and eventually, he found a job that would pay enough for him to move out of his parent's house and get on with his life. He always described it that way, as his parent's house, as if on some level he had always known that he wasn't truly welcome there.

The local police academy was excited to have an army veteran and crack-shot marksman join their training staff. He was still young, so he was only granted the title of assistant drill instructor, but there were several of his older hunting buddies that had risen through the ranks and settled into decision-making positions who were delighted to see their young friend finally dedicating his time and talents to something worthwhile.

For his part, Robert was profoundly unhappy. While he had clawed his way out of his father's shadow and begun to build a life for himself, the rage had not abated. Perhaps things would have been different if the world had been at war and his time in the army filled with danger and slaughter, but Robert had been born into a peaceful time and could find no acceptable outlet at all for the anger inside of him. In spite of managing to find a place for himself where his skills were put to good use and he was appreciated, he still could not surmount the feeling that the world had been unfair to him. To say that he had a chip on his shoulder would have been a vast understatement. He felt like the whole universe was out of balance, and that if nobody else was going to, then he needed to be the one to put it right.

Yet, just as he was building himself up to do something truly horrific, to get even with the world that had wronged him, something distracted him. Before he had left for the army, he could not get the time of day from any of the girls in town. They all knew him from school. They knew him as a pathetic joke of a boy who stuttered and was covered in spots. But in his absence and with the passing of years, a whole new crop of datable young women was starting to emerge who had no memory of him whatsoever. Teenagers, most of them fresh out of school or just finishing up their final year, who looked at a man in uniform who was praised for his military service and marksmanship medals as something of a catch.

For Robert's part, he discovered that when a girl was barely older than a child, he didn't have nearly so much nervousness to work through to speak to her. These weren't just girls who didn't know anything about him, they were girls who didn't know anything about the world in general. Sheltered and coddled by their conservative families, who viewed an older man like Robert taking their daughter under his wing as a purely positive thing. He was twenty-one years old when he married a seventeen-year-old girl with the family's consent. She had scarcely been involved in the conversation at all. He had romanced her as much as he was able and proposed to her, but most of the nitty-gritty of the arrangement had been worked out directly with her father, and after the two were wed, they moved into Robert's one-bedroom apartment together.

Married life was not really what either of them expected. Robert was fairly set in his ways, intent on carrying on doing things the way that he'd always done things, though he did have a great many expectations of his wife that would have seemed fairly unreasonable to anyone who hadn't grown up with a strict authoritarian father. His meals were to be on the table at the correct time, his wife was to be available to him sexually as and when he demanded, and he demanded extremely frequently, at least at the start of their relationship, before the 'honeymoon period' came to its abrupt end.

It is difficult to say whether either one of them was truly happy in the relationship, or if they had just carried on with it because of the expectations of society. It is also difficult to say whether or not, given time, Robert might have opened up about the trauma of his past and learned to grow past it. They would never have the opportunity to find out.

While Robert now had a sexual outlet for the first time in his life, he had expected it to solve all of his problems, and the fact that it hadn't was a cause for concern and frustration.

This wasn't how it was meant to be. He was meant to be a man, to get a job, to get a house, to marry a woman, to have sex with her. This was meant to fix everything broken inside him. This was meant to make it all right. All the insults and the laughter, he was meant to forget all of that now, but it was still there. It wouldn't go away. It just wouldn't get out of his head, no matter how much he did what he was meant to do. No matter how many times he kissed his wife goodbye in the morning, or had sex in their marriage bed, or fired a gun at the range and got a bullseye, or barked orders that were immediately obeyed, none of it made the feeling go away. The feeling that he wasn't good enough, that he was a joke, that the minute he looked away his wife's soft smile would turn into a mocking sneer at this joke of a man that she'd married. His stutter began to resurface more and more as his fear and frustration mounted. This was meant to make him right. Why wasn't it making him right?

All the old resentments that he'd expected to fade away as he settled into married life and matured just seemed to be getting worse. His fresh-faced teenage wife seemed to only exacerbate the problem. He'd been attracted to her in no small part because she reminded him of all the girls that wouldn't give him the time of day back when he was in school, but now she just served as a constant reminder of that miserable time in his life.

He had gotten exactly what he wanted, and he hated it. Everything that he'd been told would make his life better just seemed to make it worse. Every time he looked at the pretty little wife that was meant to cure him but couldn't, he grew increasingly furious. He had been betrayed over and over again throughout his life, by his father, by the school, by the kids that were meant to be his friends, and now she was betraying him too. The one person who was meant to undo all of that hurt wasn't. She obviously knew how, otherwise he wouldn't have married her to start with, so she was withholding his cure for no reason except spite.

More frequently than could be believed, in the brief span that they were married, one of his police buddies would show up at the door and give him a warning to keep it down. It was the start of the 60s by this point, progress was marching on ever so slowly, but beating your wife was still considered to be one of the perks of being a husband, particularly among the kind of men that Robert spent his time with. The pretty young face that had drawn him to her to start with was marred with bruises. The house was never kept to his exacting standards. She couldn't cook a meal without burning it or seasoning it like some Mexican. Nothing was ever right. She wouldn't even look him in the eye anymore. Wouldn't give him a kiss on the cheek before he went off to work without him grabbing her by the hair. Wouldn't reach out for him in the dark of night, in fact, she only tolerated his touch until he was done and then rolled away as quickly as she dared. All the little kindnesses that she'd shown him when they were first married had eroded away until they were just two people who didn't particularly like each other, stuck under the same roof. And worst of all, she wasn't fixing him. Damn her to hell, why wasn't she fixing him?

And so, once again faced with a world that filled him with rage and there being no end in sight, Robert began to spiral deeper into madness. Thoughts of vengeance on everyone that had ever wronged him filled his mind. He had dreams that he was out in the woods, stalking his prey, and when he looked down the sights of his rifle, there was some girl or another that had turned him down, that had laughed at him, that had rejected him, the way his wife was rejecting him now. His stutter came back in full force, making it increasingly difficult for him to do his job, making him the subject of mockery among the students at the police academy, even making his wife giggle when he couldn't force out a word. She'd giggle and giggle and he'd shut her the hell up.

There was only one way out of this that made any sense to him. Only one way for the books to be balanced so that he could move on. He had to get revenge. He had to set right some of the wrongs that had been done to him so that he could feel like he was building his life on a foundation of solid ground instead of quicksand. Even *he* could recognise that his ongoing degeneration was a result of the terrible childhood he had been through, where others might have suggested that he try to make peace with his past, Robert fully intended to make war instead.

The first blow that he struck against his imagined oppressors was not toward his father, though one would have thought that man would have been at the centre of any plans for vengeance that Robert might concoct. Chris still loomed too great in his mind. He was too powerful to attack directly. So, Robert moved on to a secondary target, one that felt more possible to take on and defeat.

On December 7th, 1960, Robert was arrested.

In the week prior to his arrest, the police had been working with locals to identify the arsonist who had destroyed the Pocahontas County school bus garage. Despite searching high and low for anyone else that they might be able to fix the blame to, there was overwhelming eyewitness testimony that placed Robert at the scene of the crime. Furthermore, he had been easily identified by the clerk at the local gas station where he had purchased the accelerants that he meant to use for the crime. There was no question that Robert had done it, but what nobody could understand was why. From the outside looking in, he seemed like a young man with a promising future. A career, a wife, a life that many would have envied. Yet he threw it all away for no reason that anyone could make any sense of.

If they had known how Robert saw the world, it might have made a little more sense. The school bus had been a focal point for his bullying and misery in high school. Every morning he had ridden it, and every morning he had faced an endless litany of rejections from everybody he tried to sit beside. Nobody had wanted him near them. They didn't want to be tainted by association with a greasy, stuttering nobody. Whoever did end up being forced to sit by him would either berate or ignore him to the best of their ability to make sure that everyone knew that the situation was not by their choice. And he lived this same horrible rejection over and over, two times a day, five days a week, for years.

He couldn't kill all the people who had wronged him so he couldn't truly set things right. But he could destroy the vehicle in which he had been trapped to suffer through countless humiliations and degradations. It was a statement of intent more than a crime of passion. He meant to burn away his entire past if he could.

This would mark Robert's first stay in prison, but it would be far from the last. He was sentenced to three years in Anamosa State Penitentiary but would ultimately only serve twenty months before being released for good behaviour.

Two pivotal events in Robert's life occurred while he was imprisoned, one of which happened almost entirely outside of his awareness, and the other was unavoidable. Within a few months of his incarceration, his wife had filed for divorce. Given that Robert was currently in prison for a violent crime, it was not at all difficult for her to get that divorce pushed through the courts quickly and cleanly with full support from both her own family and the Hansens, who mostly wanted this latest embarrassment from Robert to go away as quietly as possible.

The second event of interest proved pivotal in securing Robert's early release from jail. The prison had a psychiatric doctor on staff, meant to work with those in the prison population who were obviously suffering from some mental illness rather than simple criminality. The fact that Robert had such a promising and upstanding life prior to his arrest made him prime material for that psychiatrist. Nobody could understand why he had committed his crime, there seemed to be no logical basis for his actions, so a full psychiatric analysis was undertaken.

Robert had never had anyone in his life that he'd felt he could speak freely with about how he felt or what he thought. His father had seen to that early on by severely punishing the boy for even the smallest hint of 'complaining.' Beyond his family, Robert had never been close enough with anyone to feel comfortable sharing his private thoughts. He never let his guard down, even with his wife, because he felt that he had to constantly play the part of the ideal husband to ensure that she didn't immediately slip through his fingers. He was careful to say exactly what he thought he was supposed to say, or at least, exactly what he felt his father would have said. With the prison psychiatrist, he finally had the opportunity to open up a little about his unhappy childhood, about the root causes of so many of the problems that plagued him. In turn, the psychiatrist was able to develop a fairly in-depth understanding of Robert.

First and foremost, he was diagnosed with an infantile personality obsessed with getting back at people who had wronged him. This much was apparent as soon as the cause of his crime was revealed. But beyond that, the doctor identified two distinctive sets of mental health issues that he believed were the root cause of Robert's self-destructive behaviour. His moods swung wildly as he alternately focused on the present or allowed memories of his past to consume him. These mood swings led to a diagnosis of manic depression but even that did not fully account for his actions.

When Robert underwent his most extreme outbursts, the psychiatrist believed that he actually lost all connection to reality, if only for a brief period of time. He believed that Robert's mental landscape shifted so that the thoughts that normally remained in the background or hovered over reality like some ephemeral cloud would, in times of emotional stress, become the only perceptions he recognized and acted on. This was tantamount to hallucination, in the doctor's opinion, so he considered Robert's most extreme psychotic breaks to be a result of periodic schizophrenic episodes brought about by his traumatic childhood.

Both of these conditions were being treated pharmacologically by 1960, and the doctor was quick to propose an early release of Robert on the assumption that he would be given access to the medication necessary to manage his condition and keep himself on an even keel. This was pivotal in securing his early release from prison, even though there was no legal component to the diagnosis that would force Robert to actually take the medication that he was being prescribed.

As such, when Robert was released back into the world with the stigma of being an ex-convict now attached to his name, he elected not to add the additional stigma of being mentally ill. Pretending that he had received no such diagnosis, and actively resisting any attempts at treatment.

Everywhere he went in Pocahontas, he encountered people who knew him. People who had tormented him throughout his childhood, schoolmates, teachers, family, or strangers who had learned about what he had done and looked down on him in judgment. It became clear to Robert that the situation in town was untenable. He was never going to be able to move on with his life if he remained here. He was never going to be able to escape the swirling vortex of his past unless he got away from its epicentre.

Without work, Robert struggled to make ends meet. The police academy obviously wasn't going to employ an ex-convict, and while no law had yet been passed barring convicts from owning firearms, his criminal history made anyone who might employ him for his skill with a gun or bow uncomfortable, meaning that his only real area of expertise was denied to him too.

Technically, he might have been able to go back to working at his father's bakery, given that he still had all of the prerequisite skills and training, but his father never extended the invitation, and Robert had not yet sunk so low as to go begging.

Instead, he did what most criminals do after a period in prison has robbed them of their ability to seek gainful employment. He turned to crime. Over the next few years, he was arrested multiple times for petty larceny, serving short prison sentences each time and repeatedly setting back his plans to get the hell out of town. Every penny that he put towards his legal defence was one less to buy a ticket out of town, and nobody else was going to help him.

Or at least, that was what he firmly believed until he met Darla Henrichsen for the first time. Where everyone else looked at him with contempt, she looked at him with pity. She was a profoundly religious young woman, who often confided to others in her prayer circle that she could hear the voice of God speaking to her, and it seemed that God saw something in Robert Hansen that others did not. He may have been increasingly rough around the edges following his time in and out of jail, but underneath the acne scars, he still looked boyish, for the most part. Perhaps that was what drew her to him, this idea that innocence might still have been there lurking under the surface. She put her trust in him when nobody else would, and to Robert's surprise, he came to trust her too.

He began attending church, at her behest, and while the other congregants were less than pleased to have a man like him amongst them, Darla was quick to remind everyone that it was not man's place to judge others. And that forgiveness was the core tenet of their faith. Most of the other people that Robert met through Darla would never actually show him any forgiveness or faith, but he soon came to realise that he didn't need it. Darla was enough.

She was surprised and delighted when, after beginning to get his life back in order, he approached her with an engagement ring. It seemed like something out of a romance novel. The downtrodden man getting his life back on track for the love of a good woman. So of course, she accepted.

In 1963, they were wed. It was a smaller ceremony than Robert's first marriage and far less well attended by people on either side of the aisle. Many felt that Darla was making a terrible mistake in putting her trust in this man. He was, after all, an ex-convict with a strange stutter and cold demeanour.

For a time, life was quite tolerable for Robert. He found work in another bakery in town where he stayed behind the scenes and did the hard physical work while people without his chequered past dealt with the customers. It was here that Robert discovered that he actually enjoyed the profession that had been forced on him by his father as long as he didn't have his father hanging over him. Standards were still exacting, but nowhere near to the level that he had been accustomed to, and without constant abuse and badgering he soon came to realise that he was actually a very competent baker, capable of markedly more than most of his colleagues in no small part thanks to the training from hell that he had suffered through.

Darla was not the wilting flower of his first wife. If he tried to give her the slightest bit of grief, she stood up to him, and she made it abundantly clear from the beginning that at the first hint that he might raise a hand to her, she would be gone. She would tolerate none of the behaviour that ruined his first marriage, and she would allow him to indulge in none of his worst habits. Every time he tried to sink into his rage, she was there to drag him out, forcing him to help out at the church, or mow the lawn, or to go hunting with his friends. She actively encouraged him not only to fill his life with hard work, as his father had always tried to, but to fill his free time with fun. They were a good match, in as much as anyone could be for Robert, and this constant push to be a better version of himself based on his own standards, rather than those set by his father, was a big part of that.

Over the course of their first three years of marriage, things went better than anyone could have hoped, even if one-half of the couple did have God speaking to her directly to guide her actions. They had two beautiful, healthy children, and were raising them well. The four of them attended church every Sunday, the only hard and fast demand that Darla made on Robert's time. She was firmly convinced that the only way to keep him on the path of righteousness and away from any temptation to sin was through regular church attendance, and so, just like her hardline on abuse, so too was she firm on this. Even if it was hunting season and the other men were going out for the whole weekend, Robert would be back in town by Sunday morning, dressed in a suit and ready to go. Beyond that, he had complete autonomy. Darla never questioned him on where he went or what he did with his time, so long as she could see that he was contented, and so long as he came back to her at the end of it. It was basically the perfect marriage for Robert as he was divorced from all the bothersome demands of his previous marriage, both in terms of demands on his time as well as on his finances. Darla worked with mentally disabled children, tutoring and assisting them, and she had built herself a sizeable enough client base in Pocahontas that, in truth, Robert didn't need to work at all if he didn't want to. But it filled his time and kept his hands occupied. It also gave him a sense of purpose that she knew he would otherwise be lacking. The extra money coming into the house didn't hurt either, even though Darla never asked for a penny of it.

Despite all of this, she could see how unhappy Robert was despite his apparent contentment. He kept himself busy, and kept his mind from turning to dark thoughts, but they were still there, just beneath the surface, waiting for the slightest excuse to surge up and consume him. Every time somebody spotted him and whispered, she could feel him flinch. Every time somebody laughed, he ducked his head as if it were directed at him. Despite everything good in their life, the shadow of his past still hung over him, and she wanted to give him some reprieve from that. To take him away from this place, haunted by the memories of his lawless and miserable past, and start anew.

Together they had managed to pool enough money for them to start their new life somewhere far away from Pocahontas. As far away as they could physically get from his past, his family, and everything else that had brought him so much misery.

There was a new 'gold rush' about to begin in Alaska. A trans-Alaskan oil pipeline had finally been approved by Congress, and anybody who was anybody was rushing to get their share of the money that would soon to be flooding the state. Everyone with any experience in construction was shipping up there, and the population of every town along the pipeline would be booming within a few months. And with the construction crews would come their families, and all of the associated hangers on. Drug dealers, prostitutes, all the usual crowd that were attracted to people who had suddenly come into more money than they knew what to do with. Given this sudden growth in population, Alaska would now need people like Robert and Darla. Bakers to feed the families of the workers, and carers to help raise those children that would struggle in a traditional school environment. The pipeline represented hope for a better future for so many people, why couldn't it mean the same for the Hansen family?

More importantly than all of that though, was the fact that Alaska was also a place where nobody would be asking too many questions about anyone's past. The sort of place ex-convicts dream of, where their past was prologue and who they were in the here and now was all that mattered. In Alaska, nobody would care that Robert had set a fire or robbed a few folks, or that he'd suffered from a stutter in school and had an overbearing father. They could leave all that stuff behind and start a new life together completely fresh, like all their sins were being washed away in a baptism of snow. The thought of that appealed to Darla as much as the promise of escape from his past appealed to Robert. They sold off most everything that they had in Pocahontas, loaded all their remaining belongings into a plane, and never looked back.

The Great White

The Hansen family arrived in Anchorage in 1967 and soon established themselves in the town. Robert opened his own bakery, which was soon doing booming business, and while Darla had far fewer clients up there, her income was still more than sufficient to cover the rent on their home. The children were young enough to be resilient, and adapted well to the new climate, making friends easily in a way that Robert had never been able to, and they soon found a church to attend each Sunday that suited Darla's exacting standards.

From the beginning, her primary concern was not for the children. They were good kids, smart kids, she knew that no matter what Alaska threw at them they'd bounce back better than before. Darla's only worry in all her life was Robert. He had found something akin to equilibrium back in Pocahontas, in a place where he was under the watchful, if judgmental, eye of the community. Up here, he had no community, and where down south his peers had all been upstanding citizens in their own right, the men up in Alaska were a different breed. Just as nobody asked about Robert's past, neither was anyone allowed to ask about theirs, and Darla found herself perpetually suspicious to the verge of paranoia about what exactly these 'gentlemen' might lead her husband into. He had her, and he had the church, and he had his bakery which he'd rarely speak of, but which always seemed to fill him up with a sense of pride and accomplishment. Just like his father before him, he owned his own business, and he was making it work.

Increasingly, their paths would not cross until the evening. He rose before everyone else in the house to go and get the ovens up to heat and the bread baking, but sometimes Darla would stir in the dark of night, long before he had any cause to be away and find that the bed was empty beside her. She asked him about it, only once, because once was all she really dared. If he was off whoring or drinking or any of the other awful things he might have had free reign to do up here, she was sure that she didn't want to hear about it. But he had told her that he took himself for a hike out into the woods most mornings before work. He was getting familiar with the terrain, he said, before he started going out on hunting trips.

It was as good an excuse as she might have hoped for, and at least some part of it was soon proven true when he had finally made enough friends around town to secure himself an invite to go hunting with them. Sure as he might have been about his skills with the rifle and bow, that didn't mean he fancied his chances out in the Alaskan wilderness without a little bit of guidance. Yet despite that initial trepidation, he was soon heading out on solo hunting trips every weekend, before the crack of dawn.

While there had been hunters down in Pocahontas, and Darla had known that Robert was one of the better ones, she had never known just how good he could be until he was up here in a land where such skills weren't just properly appreciated, but treated as the highest one might hope to achieve. Just a few trips out hunting had Robert accepted into the community in a way that she couldn't have hoped for in her wildest dreams. Soon, everyone in town was coming around the bakery, just to chat with Robert about the next time they were going out. Asking him for pointers.

What had made him strange and an outcast in Pocahontas made him a hot property in Alaska. And while he was still quiet and sullen a lot of the time, so were most of the men around these parts. If Darla had taken *up* with Robert here, she wouldn't have been getting worried looks or none-too-subtle hints that she could do better, he would have been considered a catch. A real man's man, able to put dinner on the table with nothing but skill and a bullet.

He went from being an outcast to being the most beloved member of the community. When hunting season was in full swing, he came home having set new records for hunting in the region. Records in the sense that they were recorded in record books. In particular, he set a great many for bow-hunting long before it was fashionable. He did not argue from the modern position of claiming it was more sportsmanlike to hunt with a bow, but instead emphasised the silent nature of the weapon in comparison to the gun. He could down a Dall sheep without scaring a moose twelve feet away when using a bow while his competitors out in the wild would lose any chance of a kill for the whole day if they misfired. For bigger animals, he would still switch to a rifle to ensure a clean kill on the first shot, but most of the time, he would walk off into the woods in silence, remain in silence for hours, and then return with more game than his family had any hope of using, much of which was donated through the church to families that were having more trouble securing their meals.

Remarkably, his incredible talent didn't even seem to ruffle the feathers of the existing top hunters of the region, in part because he was no sort of braggart, in comparison to the majority of them, and in part because it was clear that he hunted for the sheer love of the hobby more than anything else. It only made sense that a man who lived and breathed hunting would be good at it.

The charitable donations and his willingness to help teach youngsters better marksmanship also definitely helped ensure his standing in the community, but ultimately his appeal was simply that he was a man who was extremely competent.

Darla soon saw a marked improvement in her husband's moods. He seemed to be more calm now. That had been the whole purpose of them moving up here of course, but this relief he was experiencing hadn't been instant. It hadn't been the moment that they were away from his bad memories, or the moment that he'd established his own business or the moment that he'd been accepted into the community. It had been gradual at first, fleeting moments of peace here and there that would pass so quickly she dared not comment on them. Then one day, after he had returned from hunting, she finally recognised that peace as something quite similar to a feeling she had experienced in her own life. It was how she felt after she had been in church, or after God had spoken to her. It was that sense that all was right in the world. That she was following God's plan for her. That in the end, her soul was bound for heaven.

For Robert, roaming the woods of Alaska was a transcendent experience, it was a religious rite, and each hunt that he went on was a pilgrimage.

If it had just been the killing that got him this way, she probably would have worried. But there were many days that he came back home blissed out and peaceful with absolutely nothing to show for his time out in the woods at all. It was just the peace of the woods, or so she thought, that was washing away all his sorrows and sins.

They were, to all appearances, an extremely successful family. Darla's work paid all the bills, so everything that Robert's booming business made was a bonus. This meant that when he wanted to spend a little of that money on his hobbies, he could. Darla's worries over her husband's soul persisted, she knew that there was some part of him that was drawn to crime and sin. She truly believed that only by filling all the hours that God gave him was he able to avoid succumbing to that temptation, so when he asked if it was alright to spend money on a new rifle, a new bow, a little shack out by the Knik River that he could use for hunting, she was delighted to say yes, time and time again.

The only problem arose when he wanted something but the money wasn't there. He wouldn't take any of Darla's savings, insisting that their finances remain entirely separate, but as successful as the bakery was, the cost of living in Alaska continued to climb as localised inflation resulted from the influx of wealthy pipeline workers. Housing prices climbed, as did the rent and rates on the bakery, and that put a pinch on the booming success of their early years in Anchorage.

Crime had always been Robert's fall-back position when he was in times of financial struggle, but he wasn't exactly struggling now. He was in a new position of being perfectly comfortable, but wanting more money just because he wanted another luxury to treat himself with.

All of his success as a hunter had led to him accumulating no small number of trophies. Items that he didn't much care about personally but displayed in his home all the same because they seemed to make Darla and the kids so proud of him. The trophies were actually valuable but Robert knew nobody would buy them should he try to hock them and, to him, that robbed them of their value. He needed a plan.

One day when the earth wasn't frozen too solid, he went out into his backyard and dug a hole. Wrapping all his trophies in an old bedsheet that had been set aside to make scraps, he placed them at the bottom of that hole and then buried them. From there, it was simple work to stage a break-in, he'd committed enough of them through the years.

He filed a police report, even though It made him intensely uncomfortable to be in the station and his stutter almost overcame his ability to communicate at all. From there filing an insurance claim was a far easier matter. Handing over the details of the missing trophies, marking down the cost to repair the damage he'd done to the house in the process of staging the break in and sending off the forms with the police report number attached were simple matters, especially since he'd already collated all the information that he'd need in advance.

When the cheque arrived, it barely had time to be cashed out into his account before he was off spending it. He purchased a Piper PA-18 Super Cub prop plane that would allow him to travel far out into the expansive wilderness for hunting expeditions, to easily reach his cabin by the Knik River, and to make all the money that he'd already invested in getting his pilot's license worthwhile.

The plane just added to his popularity in town of course, and all the kids desperately wanted Mr Hansen to take them out into the wilderness with him on one of his hunting trips.

He did take some of the older girls on little excursions into the woods, mostly the ones between sixteen and eighteen. When they got home they had nothing to say about the experience, didn't even mention that it had happened. For all that, it was the new American frontier, values in Alaska were pretty conservative, and if word got around that they'd seduced a married man, that would have been the end of their reputations. Or at least, that was what Robert had explained to them after he raped them. He told them it was obvious to everyone who had seen them what the girl was after when she approached him, that no good girl with proper values and good intentions would have gone off into the woods with a grown man. The girls, chosen for their immaturity, bought this lie hook, line, and sinker, and so for a time, Robert's other extra-curricular activity went completely unnoticed.

For her part, Darla was finding the adjustment to life in Alaska a little more difficult. She had been born in Arkansas, a far warmer and drier place, and struggled greatly with always being cold and with the long dark nights of Anchorage. Likewise, she felt like her kids were growing up too pale and isolated from everything that she had considered to be normal. So, each summer after their first in Alaska, Robert would happily provide funds for her to take the kids on a long vacation. Normally this several-month-long trip would be to stay with her family in Arkansas, but a few summers were spent in more exotic locations, including a tour of Europe that she hoped might help to counter the lack of 'culture' that they were experiencing in Anchorage.

Robert could not accompany them, remaining behind in Anchorage for months at a time, entirely alone. He had the bakery to think of. There was nobody in town he trusted to run the place for him, and the staff that he employed were front-of-house staff rather than bakers themselves. He had learned from the start that there was nobody else who could meet his exacting standards, so he did not ask anyone to try. He handled all of the baking himself in the early hours of the morning and through the early afternoon when he packed up for the day. These long hours were nothing new to him of course and did nothing to discourage him from pursuing his hobbies outside of those hours. He was known to rise ridiculously early in the morning to go hunting before he started work or to head out into the wilderness after a full day in the bakery with his bow slung over his shoulder and a cold calm in his eyes.

With Darla away, he had a lot more freedom in his activities throughout the summers. And it was during those summers that the vast majority of the rapes that he committed on over 40 Alaskan women took place. The teenage girls of Anchorage had gradually gotten the impression from their peers that spending time in Mr Hansen's company wasn't the best idea, even if nothing was ever publicly stated, so he had moved on to assaulting and raping older women. Just as he would with any prey, he took the time to stake out these women in advance, learning the patterns of their movements, identifying when they would be at their most vulnerable, and then moving in to strike.

In December of 1971, Robert identified a forty-one-year-old housewife living in South Anchorage as his next victim. After taking some time to identify her patterns of behaviour, he approached her at her door when she was returning home from work and brandished a .22 calibre pistol to ensure her silence and compliance as he forced her into her apartment. Inside, he pushed her into the bedroom and attempted to rape her, but she fought back, kicking at him as he tried to get between her legs and pushing him off the bed to land with a heavy thump. Almost immediately, he could hear neighbours in the other apartments talking and moving in response to the loud noise. He panicked and fled the scene of the crime.

Frustrated by his failure to rape one woman, he spent a day or so simmering, waiting to see if any repercussions would arise as a result of his actions. When it seemed that nobody was going to stop him, he went out again to look for a new victim and found a prostitute who was plying her trade to the trans-Alaskan pipeline workers outside of a bar. Offering her $300 for oral sex, a frankly ridiculous sum given the going rate at the time, he quickly secured her company in his car. When she began performing the act, he drove quickly to his house, a blue-grey ranch-style building that was set back a distance from the road, ensuring that any noises wouldn't be heard. When she objected to his driving while she was engaged in her business, he brandished a pistol at her and told her to keep going.

Once they were in an isolated enough spot, he announced that he had changed his mind, and forced her into the back seat where he proceeded to rape her at gunpoint. With his lust sated, he kicked her out of the vehicle without payment and drove off.

Both of these women would approach the police separately to tell their tales of a small, stuttering man who had attempted in one case and succeeded in the other case, at raping them. Anchorage was not so big a town that there were a great many men fitting that description, and both of them identified Robert from a photograph quite easily. After all, he had never had to make any attempt to disguise himself with any of the teenagers he raped, so it had never even occurred to him that he might want to do so with adults.

By the time that he was arrested and charges were brought, his wife and children had already returned to town from a short trip down south over Christmas. He had been completely unaware that he was under any sort of investigation in the intervening time.

Both the rape and the attempted rape were going to be charged together. While he might have been able to fight one charge with his usual appearance of innocence, the two together would present more of a problem. Not to mention the effect that this was going to have on his business and family if it all got out. So, he made a deal with the prosecutor. If they would drop the rape charges, he would plead no contest to assault with a deadly weapon in the case of his attempted rape. The rape of a prostitute was always going to be a tough nut to crack for any prosecutor, and ultimately Robert had failed to rape the housewife. In light of the fact that all they had tying him to the scene was her identification of him, there was a distinct possibility that the deadly weapon charge was going to be their best chance to put him behind bars at all.

In exchange for his cooperation, Robert was sentenced to only five years in prison for his crimes, but after only six months of serving time, he was returned to Alaska on a work release programme. They needed all hands on deck in Anchorage with the ongoing expansion of the trans-Alaskan pipeline project, so they placed him in a halfway house in Anchorage where his activity could be monitored for another six months, and then let him get on with his job.

Six months of absence had an impact on his finances, of course, but the moment that the bakery opened its doors again, he was flooded with customers and well-wishers. Thanks to his plea deal, the specifics of why he had been arrested had never come out, so there was a general consensus of opinion based on what little they did know about it from his wife, that he had been charged with 'assault with a deadly weapon'. They presumed this meant that he'd pulled a gun on somebody trying to start a fight with him. Something that in his shoes, almost any Alaskan man likely would have done.

Darla knew the truth of the matter, of course, but she blamed herself. She had always known that there was a dark pull affecting her husband and that he was a man of certain lusts that needed to be sated with regularity to keep him calm and reasonable. It was her fault for leaving him alone all those months without a woman to comfort him at night that had led to him acting out that way, but she knew that through God, he would be redeemed. Confessing to his crimes and throwing himself upon the mercy of the court had been the right thing to do, in her opinion, and she felt that God would most assuredly forgive Robert too, if he were to come to church with her each Sunday.

For a time, he did.

He behaved himself admirably while staying in the halfway house, leaving only to work and to attend church, and before long he was released entirely from the restrictions placed upon him and returned to the family home.

Throughout his time in prison, Darla and the kids had driven down every single weekend to see him during visiting hours. Six months of weekends, with her cheeks burning with shame as she had to walk past all the people at the prison who knew what her husband had done. Darla felt it was important to bring the children along with her, and not just for the ride. Even though this part of their life was a world apart from the good and God-fearing life that she had wanted for them, it was also an abject lesson in what could happen to you if you strayed from the path of righteousness. All around her were people who had only made one foolish choice, one silly mistake, and their whole lives had come apart. There could be no greater educational tool for her children than seeing their own father so diminished in stature from being the most beloved man in town to becoming a common inmate in this living hell.

They had spoken often of his guilt, of his sorrow and how, most of all, he was upset at how he had shamed her. Not that he had tried to rape one woman, and succeeded in raping another, but that he had let her down. She had not been sure how to take that.

Even when he returned home after his time in the halfway house, she had lain with him only rarely, unable to stomach the idea of what he had done, what he had tried to do to other women just like her. She did her best to do her wifely duty as the Bible told her, but it was difficult to look Robert in the eye now, let alone any of the other things that he wanted her to do.

She had never been particularly adventurous in the bedroom, and she wondered sometimes if that had driven Robert into the arms of those other women, but she would not debase herself like that, just on the off-chance that her sin might defend some stranger's virtue. That was not how it worked. Each of us is responsible for our own choices and actions, and she would not do any of the dirty things that Robert asked for. If other women would, then let it stain their immortal souls.

If other women chose to go flaunting themselves in front of a married man until he succumbed to their wiles and followed them home and then were surprised that they had been taken up on what they'd been so freely bandying about town, that was hardly her fault, was it?

And that was to say nothing of the women who sold their dignity and their bodies to anyone who'd pay. That woman had some nerve calling her husband a rapist when she was a whore. Just because she'd been so lousy in the sack that Robert wouldn't pay her, that didn't make it rape. At worst, it was maybe theft by refusal to pay for services rendered, but since the service being rendered was illegal, she didn't think that he should have had to even talk to the police about it. The whore was the one who should have gone to jail, not her sweet boy Robert.

So, for a time equilibrium returned to the family. They spent that first summer after his release together in their family home.

Robert went out hunting often, but not nearly so often as he would have if he'd had nothing but an empty house to come back to. The bakery slowly but surely got back on its feet, with the ongoing support of the community. Any fears that they might have had that their life in Alaska was going to be brought to an early end by Robert's little dalliance on the darker side of things was soon put to rest. So long as he didn't do anything else that might ruin their lives, they were going to be just fine.

What nobody knew at that time was that he had already done something else.

Crossed

Celia Beth Van Zanten was only eighteen years old when she died. She lived in a house on Knik Avenue near Northern Lights Boulevard, in South Anchorage with three of her older brothers, while her parents resided in another home further to the north side of town. It felt like a safe way for the kids to move out, while still having family around to support them if they needed anything. The kids had always been close and looked out for one another, so to see that continuing into adulthood just made sense. At about 8:30 in the evening of December 22, 1971, she decided to make a run to the BI-LO supermarket a few blocks away for some groceries before they closed up for the night. The place shut down at 9 pm, so she had to hurry if she was going to get what she wanted before they politely kicked her back out. It was dark by the time she left the house, but it was dark almost all the time, hardly worthy of comment really. Sometime around 8:45, one of her neighbours saw her on Northern Lights Boulevard, heading toward the store, but that was the last time that she was ever seen alive. She never made it to the BI-LO. She never made it home. For two days, her brothers thought that she'd gone to their parents' place without mentioning it to them, but after some frantic phone calls, her absence was reported to the police on Christmas Eve.

On Christmas day, they found her.

Between 8:45 pm on December 22nd and her discovery on December 25th, she had been abducted, bound at the wrists, sexually assaulted, cut across the chest with a hunting knife, and dumped, still alive, into a ravine in Chugach State Park, just a few hours east from Anchorage along the Seward Highway. That same highway marked the southernmost point of the park, running alongside the Turnagain Arm of the Cook Inlet which enclosed Anchorage with water from the eastern side. It was a region that was familiar to Robert, some of his usual hunting grounds from before his plane purchase.

If by some miracle, the naked girl in the ravine had been discovered immediately, then she would have survived, but with her hands bound, she had no means of climbing up and escaping the hole in the ground, and with nobody realising that she was gone for two days, the elements had plenty of time to wear on her. At some point in the first 24 hours of her confinement in this naturally formed oubliette, she died of exposure.

There was forensic evidence found on the blue-toned body of the naked girl that in spite of her bindings and the violence that she had suffered, she had continued trying to escape from the ravine for as long as she was physically capable of movement. Her body bore the marks of these failed attempts. Cuts and scratches inflicted by the expanse of stone, dirt and ice that held her captive. The rape, and slashing her with a knife, were of course terrible, but neither could compare to the nightmarish cruelty of abandoning her out there to slowly freeze to death over the course of days. With knowledge of her own impending death driving her to hurt herself over and over again by flinging herself against the implacable stone that kept her trapped.

Meanwhile, on Robert's flight map of the region, he made his first notation. A little x marking the spot where Celia's body would be discovered. Aware of the danger in keeping such a record of his crimes, Robert hid the map behind the headboard of his marriage bed, purchasing a new one for himself for everyday use and bringing that one out only to examine during those long periods that his wife was away and he required masturbatory material.

It was not a murder in the sense that we will soon become accustomed to.

He had killed the girl after raping her, but he had done it in a cowardly fashion, without his direct involvement. He had simply dropped the girl off somewhere that she couldn't escape and abandoned her to die. It didn't require the violence or the conviction of an actual murder and provided him with some sort of moral ambiguity in which to bask. He could tell himself that he had not actually killed her, that she might very well have escaped, that she might have made her way back to town through the midwinter blizzards in this frozen land while stripped naked and with her hands bound behind her, and survived. It was a pretty unlikely scenario, but it still allowed Robert to go on about his life convinced that he wasn't a murderer.

The sad fact of the matter was that even if she had escaped and made her way back to town and survived, he probably wouldn't have cared. After all, he had committed this murder just three days after raping a prostitute and five days after his attempted rape of a housewife. At that point in history, he had no idea that there would ever be any consequences for his actions. He had no idea that the police would ever connect him to any of the rapes that he'd committed since coming to Alaska. After all, he'd been getting away with them for so long without so much as a peep from any of his victims, it seemed almost laughable that after all this time he might be confronted with repercussions.

The summer of 1972 was the summer that Darla and the kids stayed close to home, and Robert developed a sense of paranoia. He would still go out hunting and he would still work, but almost all the rest of his free time was spent with his wife and children, trying to convince them that he had reformed and could be trusted to be left alone again. He attended church with regularity, even though Darla could see that he was getting none of the peace of mind from it that it brought to her, and he kept his head down all the way through the winter.

So, when the summer of '73 came along, Darla felt quite confident and happy about leaving Robert alone again for the first time since his little slip-up. He had made a mistake, he had done penance, and she had ensured that he was well satisfied with his lot in life before she took the flight back down to Arkansas with the kids.

Megan Siobhan Emerick was 17 years old when she vanished from Seward, Alaska on July 7th of '73. She had been attending the boarding school of Seward Skill Center and was last seen by her peers departing from the dormitory laundry room. It is a matter of record that Robert Hansen was in Seward on the day that she went missing, even if nobody saw the two of them interacting at any point throughout that day.

It was assumed by the school that Megan had simply left early to return home for the summer break, but her roommate did not believe it for a moment. Nobody would leave behind all of their belongings when going home for the summer, and even the most desperate to flee wouldn't leave behind their only form of identification. Taking matters into her own hands, since the administration of the school seemed intent on ignoring one of their student's vanishing, Megan's roommate searched for three days for the girl before eventually giving in and contacting the police to inform them of her having gone missing. No trace of Megan was ever found. No body, no trace evidence of her presence anywhere, nothing.

On Hansen's map, another cross appeared. This one at a remote area of the Seward region that would only be accessible by either boat or plane. A region so devoid of any sort of landmarks that the cabin where Robert took Megan would have stood out like a sore thumb if investigators into the missing girl had ever gone to the location marked on Robert's map. Alas, they did not have access to that document at the time and years later when it was finally searched, no trace of either the temporary cabin that had been knocked up and knocked down by the hunters that used it, or of the shallow grave in which Megan had been buried were to be found. It was the first girl that Robert had physically killed for himself, using the same hunting knife that he regularly used to skin and gut the animals that he stalked. He had slaughtered her with a few quick accurate cuts, much like he would to any prey that he had taken down, but which was still suffering. He cut into her young flesh, carving through skin, breast and heart, as an act of mercy. To put her out of her misery now that he had taken her down.

Once more, he returned to his regular life completely unaltered by the experience. The bakery was open bright and early the next day, the same as it always was. He met his customers with a nod and a wave of acknowledgement when they shouted through to the kitchens in greeting. Same as any other day.

Following that, there was no great adjustment in his life or improvement in Robert's mental state that prevented him from killing again. Literally, nothing had changed for the man, yet for a period of almost two years, no evidence has been found of any other murder victims. The reason for this was not that Robert had suddenly become a reformed character, or that he had stopped his campaign of terror. The reason was that he had become more selective in picking out his victims. When he abducted women and raped them during the two years after the death of Megan Emerick, he was more careful about which ones he chose, focusing almost exclusively on women working in the sex trade or adjacent to it, women who would not be believed if they attempted to report the crime. He had learned well from his previous conviction that sex workers would be marginalised by the police to the point that they were effectively subhuman, and as such, he could do whatever he wanted with them without fear of any real repercussions even if they did attempt to report his crimes. At this early stage in his murderous career, Robert's murders were undertaken almost exclusively to prevent rape victims from reporting him, so when he was able to eliminate the risk of any reports coming back to bite him, he no longer needed to kill.

The other great advantage of preying upon sex workers was of course that all he had to do was flash some money and they'd typically follow him to whatever secluded area he pleased. The frequency of his crimes did not go down during this period, only their detection. So many new sex workers were passing through Anchorage in those two years that they never had a chance to fully communicate the danger to one another, and Robert's mild-mannered appearance, stutter, and known status as a local pillar of the community all served to make him appear innocent and guileless to the women he meant to assault.

Being certain on a practical level that they would not turn him in for his crimes was one thing, but it was not the actual reason for the women's survival, at least according to Robert himself. The women that survived his attentions were the ones that completely submitted to his will. If they fought back, if they argued with him, if he wasn't entirely convinced that they were going through with the sex for free because they were attracted to him, at least a little, then he would have killed them. This suggests that either he was markedly more delusional than the evidence shows, or that the sex workers of Anchorage were singularly talented actresses.

Yet all good things must come to an end: if you consider a massive spree of rapes to be a good thing just because they did not also end in murder. On July 15th, 1975, Robert struck again, choosing a target based on desire rather than carefully winnowing his options down to the safest and easiest to acquire. Mary Thill was a housewife in Seward. Her husband was one of the workers on the pipeline which had lured them all the way up into this most isolated and distant state. She lived on Lower

Point Road, alone for the most part, with him being off at one job site or another. Yet for all that, she was not lonely. It had been easy for such a warm and caring woman to make friends, even in the cold white north, and while she had come to rely on them, so too had they come to rely on her. It was the truest expression of community. For instance, Mary couldn't drive, but one or another of her friends would always swing by on the way into town to see if she wanted to ride along. It added a minute to their journey but made her life bearable in her husband's absence.

On the 15th, one of her friends had picked her up at home to run her into town, dropping her at the local bakery before heading off to see to her own errands. A little later, sometime between one and two in the afternoon, one of their other mutual friends spotted Mary by the waterfall that flowed past Lowell Point Road. This was the last time that she was ever seen, alive or dead. It was as though she had simply vanished.

Robert was in Seward that day, and if some sources are to be believed, he later confessed to the abduction and murder of Mary. However, there was never a body recovered or a confession recorded that could give her husband, family, and friends any sort of definite closure. A little black cross on Robert Hansen's aviation chart next to Resurrection Bay, where he allegedly dumped her body, remains the only clue as to what may have resulted in Mary Thill's mysterious and permanent disappearance.

At this point, Robert was once again losing control of himself. While he typically maintained a careful balance between his secret and public life, the two began to meld together from 1975 onwards to a greater and more obvious degree. The bipolar disorder that he had been diagnosed with during his first stay in prison was causing chaotic behaviour that ran quite contrary to Robert's usual calm and measured approach to life. His manic highs and depressive lows allowed even his slightest of whims to overtake his rational judgement and overwhelm his ability to process sensory input realistically. Such episodes of misperception were exactly what the prison psychiatrist had used as the basis for diagnosing Robert with periodic schizophrenia. In this state of altered perception, Robert was so far removed from reality that he literally could not recognise the consequences of his actions.

In broad daylight, in a Fred Meyer superstore, Robert attempted to walk out the door with a stolen chainsaw. When stopped by staff, he expressed nothing but confusion, attempting to push through them until the police arrived to take him into custody. What his intentions for the chainsaw were will never be made entirely clear, as Robert entirely forgot about the incident once his mental state had stabilised. Unfortunately for him, it stabilised with him already sitting in a jail cell with no idea of what had transpired.

While he had received a mere slap on the wrist for violent rape, stealing property of minor value from a corporation was a very different matter. His defence of having no recollection of the events for which he was being charged was promptly discarded as nonsense, and he was sentenced to five years imprisonment.

Behind bars, he began to receive the medication required to stabilise his mental state, and soon it became apparent to the medical staff of the prison that an injustice had been carried out. Contacting Robert's lawyer, they made an appeal to the Supreme Court of Alaska, arguing that the sentence that Robert had received was unjust, on the basis that he was not responsible for his actions at the time of the attempted robbery, and to everyone's surprise, none more so than Robert's, the court accepted that this was the case. Robert was released with time served on the condition that he would continue to seek treatment for his mental illness, so as to prevent events like this from occurring again.

And Robert did take the pills. He went to the doctor and got a prescription, startled by the loss of control that his wildly vacillating moods had caused, and terrified of what he might give away when he wasn't thinking clearly or making decisions competently. For a normal person, it would present a problem. For a man who habitually raped and murdered, it presented an existential threat. So he followed the rules and took the pills and acted as he was meant to. Never sinking deep into depression, but never rising to the glorious joy he had once felt. Life went from extremes to a bland grey middle ground. He was never excited anymore, never so miserable that he hoped he might die, never feeling his heart hammering and his body stilling as his prey entered his crosshairs. Everything that he had thought of as his true self had been pruned away to make him safe and stable. The medication blanketed his brain with a calming, still silence and it took him almost a full year to recognise that he hated it. He hated it with a burning passion that he just couldn't tolerate anymore. He did not want to be like everyone else. He did not want to go through life feeling only a little here, and a little there. The highs were worth the lows, and even worth the risks that came with it. He could have gone on taking his medication and maintained a stable emotional state, quite possibly never doing another bad thing in his entire life. Instead, he chose to stop taking the meds because being healthy was the same as being normal and being normal was the same as being boring, and he could not stand another day of being bored with himself.

The next of his victims has never been identified, even after all the time that has passed since he committed the murder back in 1980. Her body was discovered that year in July, buried in a shallow grave next to a power line about a mile south of South Eklutna Lake Road in Anchorage. Most of the body was already gone by the time that she was uncovered. Wild animals had scavenged her corpse thoroughly, removing most of the front half of her body which was more readily accessible given that she was buried face up. Even dental records could not be pressed into service to establish an identification because a bear or a wolf had eaten the majority of her face away, scattering her teeth to parts unknown. The only reason that anyone could prove that she had been murdered at all was sheer luck. There was a stab wound in her back, spared from predation only by the fact that it was close enough to the centre of her body that the animals had not yet reached it.

In later recounting the incident, Robert would claim he could not remember who the dead woman was. She had been either a topless dancer or a prostitute that he had paid to get into his car with him some time after he had stopped taking his medication. By his accounts she was also the first woman that he had ever murdered, so it seems moderately unlikely that he was being entirely forthcoming about everything in the interviews when these details were presented. When pressed about who she was and where she had come from, Robert would say that she had come to Anchorage from Kodiak, the big island to the south of the Cook Inlet, but police investigations and forensic evidence seemed to hint that she had originated in California, casting further doubt on the veracity of anything that he said.

Regardless, events had played out much like most of the rapes that he had conducted throughout the years. He had gotten the girl into his car with the promise of money in exchange for oral sex. They drove out of town, with him saying that he was taking her to his home, but she soon realised that they had left Anchorage. He tried to placate her, explaining that he lived further out in a cabin, they just had to go a little further. She refused. She wouldn't go any further. At which point he drew his knife and told her that she would do exactly as he said if she didn't want to get hurt.

It is possible that if events had proceeded according to Robert's plans, then what followed would not have occurred, but as they were passing through a muddy section of swamp on a desolate road, the truck became stuck. Still, under threat of violence, the girl was made to help him winch the car-free, after which she had endured entirely enough of Hansen's company and made a break for freedom.

The hunting knife that he had been using to threaten her was still in his hand; he'd always found the knife more effective somehow. Women might have understood the gun and feared it with the sensible fear of anyone confronted with a device made explicitly to kill, but the knife had a visceral quality to it. There was a fear of being shot, but there was a familiarity to the knife. Few people knew what a bullet tearing through them might feel like, but the cut was all too familiar. Everyone had been cut once in their life, remembered the sharpness, the pain. It was a familiar pain. It was natural to flinch away from a pain that you knew, even if your rational mind might have resisted the motion. With a knife in hand, Robert had been amazed at what he could get away with.

But sometimes that same familiarity could breed contempt. Once somebody had felt a blade's edge enough times, they lost the fear of it. They'd still flinch at its touch, but just the sight wasn't enough to hold sway over them. Somehow, this girl from Kodiak or California or wherever she had come from, was brave enough to see Robert Hansen draw his knife and to fight. She raked his face with her nails and elbowed the arm that was trying to grab her. He raised his voice, but she didn't hear a word that he was saying, adrenaline flooded her, rushing blood filled her ears. Fight or flight. The sight of the knife had driven rationality from her mind. Instinct and panic had seized control, and neither could be threatened into compliance or reasoned with.

She stumbled over the mud and grass, rolling over herself in her haste to get back on her feet, to start running. She turned.

Then the blade sank home.

To Robert's mind, it probably wasn't a killing blow. Despite all the times that he'd killed before, he was more accustomed to ending the lives of animals than humans. At best, he'd probably considered it a warning, at worst a disabling strike to guarantee his control over her. The idea that a blow so softly struck might kill had probably never crossed his mind. The animals he hunted were thicker of skin and muscle than any human, made more densely than the fragile prey that fell before him now. Blood loss, trauma, and shock were required to take them down if you hadn't

RYAN GREEN

managed a kill shot at the outset. The knife was used to finish them off. If he'd grazed one of the Dall sheep with a knife in the same manner, it would have been up and kicking him. A buck would have torn him open for such a love tap. But this woman fell twitching to the earth as though he'd cut an artery and was bathed in her own blood. He walked around to her, fully expecting her to take off at a sprint at any moment, thinking this was some clever gambit to get him off guard. It wasn't. She lay face down in the dirt, incapable and incapacitated. That made things easier for him.

He had taken her out somewhere quiet, far from the eyes of town, and now under the midsummer sky, he was free to do whatever he wanted to her without any possibility of interruption, even from her. She was alive, but she was in no condition to resist him.

With the rape brought to its inevitable conclusion Robert now had a decision to make, and equally inevitably he chose the cruellest possible course. Dragging the disabled woman across to what would eventually be her grave, he made her lay there as he dug. She could do nothing, overwhelmed with knowledge of what was about to happen, anticipating the nightmare to come. After the other activities of the night, he had little patience or energy for digging, so there was the small mercy that she didn't have long to wait before he grew tired of the manual labour and seized hold of her again.

For one last time, she was able to look up at the stars, bright as pinholes in the sky of the Alaskan wilderness. She was able to stare up into the infinite before her own very finite life was brought to its awful end. A patter of rocks and mud fell across her bare stomach. Then another. A heap of dirt dislodged from the side of the hole landed on her face, going into her eyes, and her mouth. She couldn't even spit it out. She could only lay there as more and more was added. More cold wet earth on her naked body. More weight pressed down on her, making it so that even if she did somehow regain control of her body and manage to

70

move, she would be pinned in place by the sheer weight of it all. One shovelful of wet, cold dirt at a time, Robert buried her alive.

Once again there were small mercies, with the bitter cold and the severity of her injuries, she might not have remained conscious long enough to understand what was happening to her. She might not have understood that she had been used like a toy and then discarded like a piece of rubbish, to be hidden from sight as if offensive to the sensibilities of the hygienic.

Whoever she had been before that night didn't matter anymore. Nothing mattered anymore. Because the earth took her all the same, and then nature took her, and then there was nothing left for anyone to recognise. No matter how many times her face was reconstructed over the years using one ingenious method or another, no matter how far forensics advanced, she would remain a mystery. Because at the end of the day, she was just another one of the faceless hundreds who passed through Alaska during the trans-Alaskan pipeline gold rush. One of the many who never made it home again to tell the tale.

After the beasts were done stripping the flesh from her bones and after she had been dug up, probed, measured, and every detail of her life scraped from her body by forensic investigators, she was buried again under the generic name of Jane Doe. The locals, and eventually the press, would come to dub her Eklutna Annie, so named for the lake she'd been buried beside. Sadly, she was now remembered only for the place and manner of her death. Everything about this once-living, breathing person who, like everyone else, once held hopes and dreams for a bright future was now forgotten, erased, and relegated to nothing more than a sombre footnote in the story of Robert Hansen.

From the perspective of Robert, this woman's death seemed to reaffirm his old suspicions that he could get away with literally anything. Her death didn't only go unnoticed, it was as though she had never existed at all. As though it had all just been a rather violent dream. As such, he was encouraged to continue down the path he had chosen rather than taking the unfortunate woman's demise as a sign that things would no longer continue to go smoothly for him.

On May 19th, 1980, Joanna Messina made a dinner date with Robert Hansen. She was a topless dancer and had met Robert during one of his many visits to the establishment where she worked. Each time he had visited, he had eyes only for her, inviting her out with him, time and time again, until finally she'd taken pity on the softspoken man and agreed. Her expectations were not high. Typically, when a man invited a topless dancer out on a date it was not because he intended to propose marriage somewhere down the line, but this guy seemed harmless enough, and if she could make a couple hundred dollars by having sex with him, then why not?

She took her dog out for a walk and then drove to the restaurant where Robert had proposed they meet. To her immense surprise, he actually took her out to dinner, paid for everything and spoke to her in his stuttering and bashful manner as though she were an actual human being. It was like it was a real date; not like she was just an object for him to consume. It disarmed her enough that once dinner was over and he invited her to come back to his place for the night in a forthright but surprisingly polite manner – without mentioning that his wife was currently holidaying abroad with their children – she had accepted before she knew it. She fetched her dog out of her car so that it wouldn't be left out overnight and climbed into his vehicle. If she had just continued to behave as if everything were a normal first date, as if she wasn't just waiting for the other shoe to drop, then maybe things could have turned out differently. Once they were in the car and on their way, however, she assumed the role she thought he expected of her and offered to have sex with him for cash.

This seemed to be the turning point in the evening for Robert. He had obviously known who she was, what she was, when he first approached her, but with her offer, he suddenly became sullen and silent and her further advances only seemed to irritate him instead of please him. The convivial atmosphere in the car had suddenly turned chilly and after only a few minutes of driving it became clear to her they were heading out of town, not to any little house in the suburbs where she could make a little cash lying on her back. She asked him if he meant to pay, he said no. She demanded that he stop the car, again he refused. There was nothing she could do short of jumping out of the moving vehicle and abandoning her dog to this man and whatever evil he might inflict upon the poor creature. She wasn't willing to suffer the pain of hitting the road or the danger of a hike back to town, even if night would still be a long time coming. And she certainly wasn't willing to leave her dog with this angry stranger who she'd taken for an easy mark.

She offered one last time to have sex with him for money and he turned her down as plainly as he'd asked her out to dinner. They trundled on along the rough roads in silence. They made their way out towards Snow River, far from the lights of town and the safety of civilisation. North and west, up backroads past Seward to the depths of the national forest of Chugach. Across the water and further on still. They were together in silence for what felt like days, but was only hours, with the dog in the backseat, nose pressed to the window and tail wagging, thinking that it was going out for a walk in the wild.

Robert stopped the car abruptly in what seemed to be just as abandoned a place as anywhere else. No landmarks or road signs gave any indication of where they might be. Then he reached past her, making her flinch her legs away, opened the glove box, and drew out a .22 calibre revolver.

We don't know if she ran at the sight of the gun, or if he forced her out of the car at gunpoint before demanding that she run for her life. Likewise, we don't know at what point the dog was released from the car, though it seems likely it came bounding through into the front seat and out into the long grass at the roadside to follow after its owner.

Whether she was already running, or Robert fired off his pistol to scare her into motion, the dog died first. A single round was all it took to kill the poor animal as it had capered after its owner. Just another animal that Robert had hunted. The same as Joanna. The same as all the rest.

He hit her a glancing blow with the first shot and had to follow it up with a second, to the centre of mass, to be sure that she was dead.

There was no sex involved in this murder. This fact made the killing distinctive from all the others. He was not killing her because he wanted to cover up a rape, he was killing her because she was a prostitute and he knew that he could get away with doing anything that he wanted to a prostitute.

From there, it was just a matter of cleaning up. Her dog and her belongings were tossed into the woods to let nature reclaim them and tidy up for him. Joanna was dragged to the gravel pit nearby and cast off the walkway along the clifftop to tumble limp and dead into the heap of gravel by the bottom. He then deliberately dislodged more gravel from uphill to spill down onto her and conceal her from sight.

Finally, Robert discarded the pistol into the Snow River itself. This was done as an afterthought but, in retrospect, was completely unnecessary. By the time that Joanna's body was finally discovered it had been quite thoroughly eviscerated by the local wildlife, leaving little trace of her identity, let alone the cause of her death.

By June, the itch was back. It had been less than a month since the last killing and Robert was already hunting again. On the 28th, Roxanne Easland told her boyfriend that she was going to meet a man downtown on 4th Avenue. It was within easy walking distance from the motel they were staying in on Spenard Road in Anchorage. They'd been there for two weeks trying to get the details of his job locked in and trying to find someplace to rent that hadn't been so overpriced by the local inflation that it would eat half his wages. Roxanne would never know the comfort of a home again and her body would never be discovered. The only reason that we know that Robert Hansen killed her at all was his confession to that effect.

There is good reason to suspect that Roxanne was the first woman that Robert deliberately released after her rape so that he could hunt her. The foundational work to plant the seeds of such an idea in his mind had already been done with his murder of Joanna Messina and her dog, and future bodies would show evidence that he had hunted them down with his rifle, but the exact moment that he began pursuing this unique sport, a moment that would have been intensely important to Robert, was never documented. Except, of course, for the fact that he confessed to the murder of Roxanne, even though there was no evidence connecting him to her at all.

The twenty-eight-year-old dancer Malai Larsen was reported missing on the 10th of July. Almost nothing is known about what happened to her, and it would take three years before her body was discovered, discarded in a parking lot like she was a piece of trash that Robert had tossed out of his car window before driving on. There wasn't enough of her left for forensics to confirm whether he hunted her the same way that he had Roxanne Easland, but given the pattern of his behaviour, it seems reasonable to assume this is what happened.

For a few months, the slaughter seemed to stop, or at least, no evidence had been found that Robert killed during those months, but by September the 6th, he was back to his old hunting grounds. Robert targeted Lisa Futrell as his next prey for the hunt. She differed from most of his other victims by virtue of her age. Until now, Robert had typically gone after teenage girls or women in their early twenties. Such individuals were young enough that they did not intimidate him, and naive enough that they were unlikely to have sufficient experience of the world that would allow them to identify him as a threat. Something had changed in Robert which now gave him the drive and the confidence to go after a more dangerous game. Most likely, it was the abrupt change in his interests from simply subduing and raping his targets to the thrill of hunting and killing them that became the primary cause for his actions. Before it had been the rape, and getting away with it, that had been the important thing, but now he had discovered a course of action that was pleasing to him in a way that simple rape was not. The hunting of women, the killing of them, these were a part of the pleasure for him now. They were, in fact, the greater part of the pleasure, and the imbalance between the enjoyment he took in carnal relations and the delight that he found in murder would continue to skew in the latter's favour for as long as his progress down this path of madness went unimpeded. At 41, Lisa was the oldest victim Robert ever went after, but he met her in an Anchorage nightclub amongst all the younger women that he usually pursued, so it is entirely possible that he just misjudged her age under the dim lights and through the haze of too much whiskey. Regardless, he managed to convince her to leave with him when her shift was over, either through the promise of money, the threat of violence, or good old-fashioned flirtation. No matter which bait he used in the snare, the result was the same. She failed to show up at work for her next shift and failed to return home at the expected time which led her younger roommates to call the police and report her missing. Her body would not be recovered for another 4 years after that report was made. When it was eventually located, it was too picked over by predators and scavengers to paint much of a picture of what had happened to her at Robert's hands. What remained of her was recovered from another gravel pit, south of what used to be the Knik Arm Bridge. Too much time had passed since her murder for her body to tell investigators any sort of story. Weather, predation, and decomposition had taken their toll. There were no clothes to be found, not even scraps, so nothing remained that could even suggest precisely what had happened to her. Nobody knew except for Robert Hansen.

For over a year after her disappearance, Robert's campaign of slaughter seems to have ground to a halt. After taking so many victims in rapid succession, the typical pattern for a serial killer would be one of continuing escalation. Based on that pattern, he should have killed more women, faster, as his addiction became more pronounced and the 'high' that he got from the murder offered diminishing returns. Instead, he seems to have switched back to being quiet and passive, picking up prostitutes and raping them without killing them while brimming with the confidence of a man who had gotten away with doing the very same thing a hundred times. It is possible that he was back on his medication during this period of time and his moods were adequately stabilised once more, but with the exception of the complete lack of dead bodies being sprinkled across the Alaskan wilderness, there is no supporting evidence one way or the other. Regardless of the underlying reason, this was another period where simply meeting up with Robert was not necessarily a death sentence for every sex worker that he encountered. This all-too-brief hiatus lasted until the second half of 1981, when he was back up to his old tricks, albeit with some refinement.

The new scheme was fairly similar to the previous, although with a bigger and more delicious bait to lure the girls in, and it promised markedly less danger to himself. Instead of seeking out women willing to prostitute themselves, Robert was instead picking girls who would be willing to pose for nude photographs for his private collection and offering them $300 for a photo session. This session was of course entirely fictional, and Robert didn't even bother to bring a camera. His intent on each occasion was to rape and murder them, so he could even use the same wad of cash over again each time.

Sherry Morrow was the first to fall for this new gambit. She was a 23-year-old topless dancer in Anchorage, who told her friends about this guy she was going to meet who was paying her $300 just to snap some nudie shots of her. She headed off to meet him on November 17th, 1981, and that was the last time she was seen alive.

Since Robert couldn't very well bring this would-be model home to a house full of his wife and kids, he took her out to the little shack that he had on the Knik River, making good use of his plane to cross the distance as swiftly as possible. Under the threat of violence, he took her inside that hut and raped her until he was satisfied, then informed her that she was going to die. He offered her one chance to survive. He would even give her a head-start. All that she needed to do was run. If she got away from him before he shot her, she got to live. If she didn't, her troubles were over.

He readied his Ruger Mini-14 hunting rifle as he spoke, checking it over and ensuring it was in the best possible working order. She reached for her clothes, but he just gestured to the door with the rifle. Not only did she have to try to run home through miles of frozen wilderness, she had to do it naked. There was a little smirk on his face the whole time. If it hadn't been for the violence that she'd already been exposed to that day, Sherry probably wouldn't have believed he was capable of this cruelty. But of course, he was.

She didn't make it far. Three gunshot wounds were found on her body, along with the accompanying casings, preserved by the snow and ice until the next year when her corpse was discovered in a shallow grave. A curious detail of this particular murder was that after she was killed and dragged to the site where she would then be buried, Robert took the time to put her clothes back onto the body. Perhaps he simply didn't want to dispose of them separately, or perhaps he was showing some sort of remorse or respect for the dead. Though given his track record, the latter seems extremely unlikely.

Just a few weeks later, the next victim fell into Robert's lap. He had such a perfect experience with Sherry that he just wanted to do it all over again as soon as he could. Andrea Altiery was a 24-year-old exotic dancer who left her friends at home, taking a taxi to the Boniface Mall in Anchorage where she meant to meet a man to pose for some photographs.

She was at least spared the indignity of being hunted. After meeting up with Robert at the mall, he threatened her with a pistol to ensure her compliance, blindfolding and handcuffing her as he forced her into his car. He drove out from town to a service road near the Knik Arm Bridge, just off the Palmer Highway, and eventually found a secluded spot to begin his evening's activities. It was now well past midnight and into the early hours of the morning. Andrea had departed from home to meet him at about 11 pm. Keeping the blindfold in place, he removed her bindings so that he could also remove her clothes and began to sexually assault her as he had all the women before. Unlike the other women, Andrea fought back, biting him and raking him with her nails until finally, she managed to get out from underneath him and run. He took her down with a single shot to the back of the head from his .22 Browning pistol, unsatisfied with how things had played out. If she had just been compliant then he could have played his game and had his fun. Now he was in a foul mood as he tied a duffel bag to her leg and filled it up with gravel from the roadside. As with most of his victims, he took a little trophy off Andrea's corpse, a distinctive fish-shaped necklace that she was well-known for. Then, having added a little bit of robbery on top of the murder and attempted rape, he dragged her to the bridge and cast her over the side into the water below. Her body would never be recovered. Even when that section of the river was trawled for remains, she was not found. It seems most likely that the duffel bag's weight was not sufficient to keep her pinned in place and she was carried away by the rushing river.

After that failure, there was another brief respite before Robert went out on the hunt again. Perhaps his failure to complete the ritual of rape and hunting the last time had left him soured to the idea of trying again, at least for a while. It certainly seems that those times that he failed to achieve his goals slowed him down a lot more than those occasions when his plans unfolded smoothly, and one might imagine that he'd have been satisfied with the outcome of his labours. Dissatisfaction had been the hallmark of his early life, and when he encountered problems, instead of pressing on to make matters better for himself, he tended to rear back from them and retreat. It isn't unreasonable to suggest that the reason he never reached the mass-murdering frenzy that characterises the end phase for so many serial killers was his tendency to retreat when failure reared its head. Each time that he began building momentum, there would be some resistance from one of his victims that would put him off, and he'd have to start building up again from the start, months later.

In May of 1982, Sue Luna agreed to a photoshoot for one of the clients of the exotic dancing club where she worked. Just like Sherry Morrow, he took her by plane, at gunpoint, out to the Knik River, and he hunted her with his rifle as though she were an animal, stripped naked and terrified. He hunted her through the forest, shot her down and buried her by the side of the river. As it was summer, the ground was soft enough for such things to be possible. So far as we can tell from the remains discovered, this particular hunt was a complete success, and Robert got everything that he wanted out of the experience. As such it should come as no surprise that the hunt started anew only a short while later.

Tamera Pederson last spoke to her family on August 7th, telling them on a phone call that she'd been offered money to pose for some photographs. She was an exotic dancer, so the kind of photographs she'd be asked to pose for were obvious to everyone involved, but they were polite enough not to mention her new foray into pornography. After that phone call, it was as though she had fallen off the face of the earth. Nobody saw her or heard from her again until many years later when Robert Hansen pointed to the spot where she had been buried on a map, about a mile and a half from the old Knik River Bridge. Once again, everything seemed to go perfectly to his designs, so it was not long before he found the courage to try again.

Angela Lynn Feddern was last spotted by someone that knew her on Fourth Avenue in Anchorage in February of 1983, but she would not be reported missing until May. She was an exotic dancer at a nightclub, and it was only because her employer had noticed that she'd been missing shifts that the police were ever informed of her disappearance. Robert had taken her out to a small body of water just off the Figure Eight Lake, having flown right around the Gulf of Alaska with her before finally killing her. This was the only time that Robert was known to have travelled so far to hunt and kill, but it suggests a worrying larger picture. If he was willing to travel 126 miles from his usual hunting grounds, it is entirely possible that there were a great many more women that he abducted and killed, leaving them scattered so far across the Alaskan wilderness that they have never been found, or at least never connected back to him.

DeLynne Renee Frey was last seen in March but wasn't reported missing for many months due to having lived a rather erratic lifestyle with a great deal of travel, irregular working hours, and many other factors. That early in the year, the ground was not soft enough for Robert to properly bury her, so she was discovered in August exposed to the elements on a sandbar in the Knik River by a pilot. She would not be identified until 1989 when an Alaskan State Trooper recognised some of her jewellery from a case file. Until then she was buried as a 'Jane Doe' in Anchorage Cemetery.

Teresa Watson left her friends behind on March 25th, informing her roommates that she was off to make a quick $300 in exchange for a couple of hours of work. Robert took her to Scenic Lake before raping her and then setting her loose to run naked through the freezing temperatures. Due to a recent cold snap, the ground was too hard for him to dig even a shallow grave for her, so he simply left her where she had fallen and headed home to the warm embrace of his completely oblivious family.

Paula Goulding was a 30-year-old exotic dancer, taken on April 25th of the same year, just a day after Malai Larsen's body was discovered in a parking lot near the Knik Arm Bridge, and just a few weeks after Watson and Frey's demise. Following the same routine as always, he offered her money for her company, then drove her to the airfield. When she was unwilling to get onto a plane with him, he drew a gun on her and forced her into handcuffs before physically carrying her to the plane and throwing her inside. Once they reached a sufficiently remote location, Robert touched down and attempted to rape her. She fought back as viciously as she could manage while still shackled and did succeed in stopping him for a while. Unlike other occasions when Robert would have become flustered by her resistance and the whole thing would have gone awry, he managed to maintain his cool, eventually stripping her, and then setting her loose to run as he hunted her down with a .223 calibre rifle. He dressed her again after her death and buried her in a shallow grave by the side of the Knik River, as he had so many before her.

Robin Pelkey was only 19 when she went missing in July. Only partial skeletal remains of her were found, but the injuries on them indicated that she had been shot down and then finished off with a knife much like a hunter might end their hunt. The parts that turned up were discovered near Palmer, further northeast than Robert usually hunted his women, so it is possible that Robin made it further than most before being caught. It is also entirely possible that she was not one of Robert's victims at all. She may have simply been an unfortunate woman who happened to have been murdered by someone else during the same time period. In addition to her having been hunted further out than most of his victims, there was another key factor that differentiated this murder from his others. While all of Robert's other victims in this period were exotic dancers or sex workers, there is no evidence that Robin was involved in the trade, but that may simply be because there is scarcely anything known about her beyond the fact that she lived in Anchorage for a few months prior to her disappearance. She would not even be identified until 2021 when one of her relatives took a DNA test for genealogy purposes. The information was shared with the police as a matter of course and genetic markers flagged up against samples taken from her remains.

Seventeen girls were all slaughtered by a man who looked and behaved for the most part like a completely harmless, inoffensive nobody. The town of Anchorage was flooded with minor criminals and tough-looking men during the pipeline gold rush, and yet Robert faded unnoticed into the background. All day long these women were confronted with men who were outwardly dangerous and they had almost all learned to be wary of them, but Robert didn't look scary at all. His appearance didn't set off any warning bells. His stutter and his soft-spoken nature didn't raise any red flags. Everything about him made him the perfect predator, hidden in plain sight and completely escaping attention because he was so very normal. He had spent every moment in Alaska being completely underestimated by everyone. When he had first started hunting, nobody in their right mind would have guessed that this meek little suburban baker might develop into one of the most efficient killers that the state had ever seen, securing awards for his talents. Likewise, none of the women who would normally have known to avoid danger took him to be any sort of serious threat, and every one of them had paid for that mistake with their lives.

The Last Hunt

Cindy Paulson was the last known girl that Robert ever picked up with the intention of playing his perverse little game. She was 17 years old and apparently possessed the kind of luck that none of the women before her had hoped for.

He had fallen back into his old habits with her, picking her up as a prostitute rather than a model on June 13th and agreeing to pay her handsomely for sex. She took him for one of the usual johns, and none of the other prostitutes working the same bars had ever given her any warning about a man of his description. Possibly because all of the prostitutes that he had raped in the past had moved on as the work on the pipeline began to slow, but more likely because nobody had ever made it back to tell tales about him before.

She got into his car, and he took her home without giving her the slightest hint that there might be any sort of problem. His house was as inoffensive and suburban as it got in Anchorage, and absolutely nothing set off any alarms for Cindy. There were signs that he had a wife and kids, but they didn't seem to be home. They were off on holiday, as they tended to be during the summer months, so she and Robert had the whole place to themselves. They had a drink together and made idle small talk on arrival, then he led her down to the basement. This was the first indication that there was anything odd going on but given just how many green flags were flapping in the breeze, Cindy didn't recognise this red one.

It was only once she was downstairs and saw the chains that she began to worry. Robert seized her by the hair, dragged her over to a supporting pillar in the middle of the room and bound her to it, forcing her down into a squat and looping a chain around her neck to pin her immobile against the pillar. As much as she flailed and struggled, once the chain was around her neck there wasn't much that she could do to escape, let alone defend herself, given the awkward position he'd trapped her in. She fought only a little, flailing and scratching at him until he hit her once. After that, she stopped dead. She remained frozen in place, like a deer in the headlights.

Taking his time, he stripped her out of her clothes, carefully folding them and setting them aside on the dusty floor. He did it all with a practised ease as if he'd done it a hundred times before. If she hadn't already been paralysed with terror, then seeing that should have been sufficient to frighten whatever remaining wits she had out of her.

From then, what followed was a mixture of sexual assault and sadistic torture. She was raped, but Robert seemed to find more pleasure in causing her pain than anything else. Trapped and utterly helpless, all that she could do was give him what he wanted and hope that when it was all over, he would let her go. Eventually, after what felt like days of this torment, Robert raped her to its natural conclusion and then staggered away.

This would be the moment that most bad johns would have felt guilt and remorse over what they'd done. After their lusts were fulfilled the clarity of realising what they had just done washed over them. But not Robert. Robert calmly dressed himself again and stood back to admire the naked woman bound in his basement with an expressionless stare that Cindy couldn't even hope to read. In the dimly lit basement, his little eyes shone black like beetle shells, completely blank and hiding whatever awful thoughts were behind them. With a nod of satisfaction, he walked over to a couch pushed up against the wall of the basement, and he lay down for a nap.

In his regular life, Robert didn't sleep. Or at least, he didn't seem to have any sleep schedule to speak of. Most nights while everyone was tucked up in their beds, he was out trawling the strip clubs and streets or roaming the wilderness hunting for the more legal kind of prey. Some afternoons after he was done in the bakery, he would take a nap, but it was always brief and restless. But this time, with his lusts slaked and the joy of the hunt still ahead of him, with everything going perfectly according to his plans, he found the kind of blissful dreamless sleep that seemed to elude him in every other part of his life. Even when Cindy sobbed or slipped and started choking on the chain around her neck, he didn't stir. If she hadn't been so terrified of what he might do if he woke up, she likely would have screamed just to see if there was anyone that might hear, even though both she and Robert knew that they were too far from any other houses for her to have much hope.

When Robert woke up hours later, calm seemed to suffuse him. All the dread that had overwhelmed her before faded from Cindy. It was over, he was calm now, rational. This was what she had expected after the violence and the rape were done, for him to transform back into the weedy nebbish little man that he was, and let her go, most likely with a wad of cash and profuse apologies over how he'd treated her. That was what she would have expected. A horrible, scary, experience, but not one that was completely beyond her usual realm of understanding. Bad johns happened. Everyone ran into them sometimes, but at the end of the day, the pain was the price of doing business. She was selling her body knowing that bad things might happen to that body in the same way that everyone working on the pipeline knew that one little industrial accident might leave them disabled for life. The risk was part of the equation, and it was why they got paid well for their services. Balance.

Robert picked up his pistol from where it had been hidden, but he was so cool about undoing her chains and directing her to get dressed, that she didn't have any real fear left of him. She could almost understand the rage that overtook people sometimes, she might have only been seventeen, but she'd lived a hard enough life to know that sometimes it got overwhelming and you needed to lash out. She didn't like that she'd been the one getting lashed this time around, but she could at least understand it. And now that the rage was gone, she should have had nothing left to fear.

She dressed herself at gunpoint with barely a quake in her hands. He should have realised she wasn't going to bolt by now, so pointing the gun at her seemed a bit needless, but maybe he was just a nervous little guy. It would explain the stutter. Once she was fully dressed, he led her back out to the car, and she wholly expected to be taken back to where he'd first picked her up off the street.

To her surprise, they headed out in an unexpected direction, travelling to Merrill Field airstrip instead of the city proper. He told her, eventually, when she was starting to become agitated, that he was taking her out to his cabin in the woods so they could spend some more time together. She had enough sense to recognise the danger inherent in this, but there was nothing that she could do about it, beyond nodding along like a good and pliant girl. This seemed to satisfy him.

He had laid her across the back seat of the car without any restraints beyond a pair of handcuffs on her wrists, sure enough in her compliance that he'd felt no need to tie her up. On arrival at the airfield, he drove right up to the side of his plane and then proceeded to get out and start loading it. He left her with a casual threat of death if she made any attempt to escape, but by this point, it was more out of habit than anything else. He felt certain that she was just going to lay there and be quiet.

Given the odd time of night, the security guard at Merrill Field became a bit suspicious about what Robert was up to and took note of his plane's tags. This would become vital later on when the police were attempting to corroborate the stories that they were told.

Gathering her courage now and recognising that there was no way that she was coming back from a flight out into the vast wilderness of Alaska beyond the safety of Anchorage, she took action.

While they'd been driving, she had been silently working the distinctive baby blue sneakers that she wore off her feet and she managed to shove them underneath the passenger's seat. She hoped that this would prove beyond a doubt that she had been in the car, just in case it came down to his word against hers, or in case he did take a potshot at her when she tried to flee. Unfortunately, that did leave her barefoot when she slipped out of the car onto the airfield tarmac. It might have been bitingly cold, sending sharp knives of pain up her heels with every step, but on the plus side, it made her movements almost entirely silent. So silent that even the master huntsman Robert Hansen, attuned to every sound around him, did not notice that she was out and running until Cindy was almost entirely out of sight.

He spotted her as she passed under one of the few lights dotted around the place, and sprinted after her, not daring to fire his gun and draw attention. Cindy ran like her life depended on it, which of course, it did. She ran, heart thumping in her ears, terror settling like a lead weight in her stomach. He was right behind her; she could hear his feet slapping on the tarmac as he ran. At any moment, he could just lift his gun and pull the trigger.

She ran until the night swallowed her up, until she couldn't think, there was nothing but the ache in her legs, the ache in her lungs, good pain, pain that told her she was still alive, no matter what he had done to her, she was still alive. And she was going to get out of this alive, no matter what it took.

The airfield was a good distance out from the city. Cindy was not dressed for the weather, had no shoes on her feet, and had already been battered around brutally earlier in the night, but all the same, she had the unyielding power of fear driving her on, and she made it all the way to Sixth Avenue where she was able to flag down a trucker passing through town.

Robert Yount was the trucker in question. Usually, he'd never pick up a hitchhiker, but he could recognise a damsel in distress when he saw one. He swerved up to the curb, and she was up and in the cabin faster than he could roll down the window to invite her in. Tears were streaming down her face, she was gasping for air and within a moment of getting in, she was shoving herself down into the footwell, trying to hide. He could hardly make out what she was saying through the sobs and chattering teeth, but he understood well enough that whatever had her so terrified was still out there, so he stamped on the gas and got the hell out of there.

As they drove, he got little fragments of her story, not enough to piece together the full picture, but enough to put the fear of God in him. He drove on ever faster through the icy night, eventually interrupting her near-catatonic sobbing to ask where he could take her where she'd be safe.

This was in the days before cell phones, so if she wanted help, she needed to find a landline. She spotted a sign for the Mush Inn and asked him to drop her there so she could call her boyfriend to come pick her up. Yount told her that what she needed to do was call the police, but for obvious reasons, Cindy was a little reluctant to get them involved. Hurting her, chasing her, trying to take her out into the middle of nowhere to kill her, those things were obviously all illegal, but so was prostitution. She had no way of knowing if the cops would listen to her whole story and go after the monster who'd tried to murder her, or if they'd get as far as her being a prostitute and lock her up for that without hearing another thing she had to say for herself.

The moment that he pulled up by the Mush Inn, Cindy was out and running again, not pausing to glance back or even to shut the door of the cabin. Yount had to get out himself and close it before looking after the girl with a sigh. Inside the Inn, she was already pleading with the clerk to call her boyfriend where he was staying at the Big Timber Motel so that he could come and get her. Yount continued on his way until he found a public phone, and then he called the police, telling them all that he knew about the cuffed and dishevelled girl that he'd rescued before heading on.

The Anchorage Police Department sent out a car as soon as they received Yount's call. Given the sheer volume of women in the sex trade who had gone missing over the past few years, this report was being treated with the respect that it deserved. But in spite of their fast action, they arrived too late at the Mush Inn. The same bored and now confused clerk was behind the counter, explaining that she had tried to call her boyfriend, had no luck, and then called a taxi to take her home to the Big Timber.

The same officers followed her over, getting her room number from the clerk and banging on the door of her room. She didn't answer, even when they said that they were the police. Eventually, the clerk had to unlock the door for them, at which point they saw poor Cindy curled up in the corner in the dark, completely alone, still shivering with terror and the intense cold, and still handcuffed. It painted a pretty unpleasant picture of what had happened to her. An unpleasant and accurate picture.

She was taken down to the station despite her protests that she didn't know anything, and slowly, laboriously, the whole story was extracted from her. They removed the handcuffs from around her wrists and stored them as evidence. From her story about the plane, they went to the airfield, and from the security guard at the airfield, they were able to get the plane tags, and Robert Hansen's name and address.

Robert had a great many run-ins with the law under his belt, so there was little doubt among the officers that he was capable of what he had been accused of, but when the police went to interview him, he categorically denied any involvement. He told them that Cindy Paulson was attempting to extort money from him, having found out about his criminal past, and was using that as a means to apply pressure on him and cause trouble. To the officer's surprise, this mild-mannered man, considered by many to be a pillar of the community, had just offered a very rational, succinct, and believable reason that Cindy might have falsely accused him and staged her own abduction. Obviously, however, Robert's word alone wouldn't be enough to entirely clear him of suspicion. So, it was lucky that he had an alibi. His friend John Henning had been with him at the time that the lying hooker was accusing him of abducting her. They had been out hunting.

An officer was dispatched to Henning's home, and John confirmed everything that Robert had said. He wasn't about to get his friend in any kind of trouble with the law. Didn't matter where Robert had been or what he had done – when the police came asking, John wouldn't say a damn thing. Just like he'd always told Robert he wouldn't. Just like they'd all agreed. Folks didn't come to Alaska, the last frontier of freedom, so that they could turn on each other and hand their friends over to the cops. They lived to a code of honour that folks down south would never understand.

A code of honour that meant that even with all the incriminating evidence, Robert was allowed to walk free after abducting, torturing, and raping Cindy Paulson with the intent to kill her afterwards.

But Cindy was not the only one that Robert had hurt, and over the course of the past few years, more and more of the bodies that he had left in his wake had been discovered. Not all of them, many never would be found, and others would only be found as future events unfolded, but enough had been discovered that there was a team put together of Alaska State Troopers with a remit to investigate. Detective Glenn Flothe proved to be the pivotal member of this team. While there were many theories put forward regarding the three dead women found in swift succession, Flothe was the one most convinced that they had a serial killer on their hands, and as such, he was the one who proceeded to treat the case the way that it deserved to be treated. Gathering up all of the evidence that could be found, he reached out to the Federal Bureau of Investigation for assistance, eventually being put into contact with what would later come to be known as the Behavioural Analysis Unit.

At the time, John Douglas – the founder of the unit, and one of the creators of criminal profiling as we know it today – was still dealing directly with cases rather than being able to delegate to people who had trained under him. As such, it was Douglas that Detective Flothe ended up in communication with. Examining all the evidence that had been gathered to date, Douglas provided a profile of the perpetrator of the crimes which was quite general in most areas, but strangely specific in others. The more common aspects could just be considered norms of serial killer psychology, like the collection of trophies from his victims, so that he could revisit his memories of killing them, but other parts of the profile were so precise that they formed the backbone of the State Trooper's investigation. Their perpetrator would be a white male, an experienced hunter with a long history of rejection by women. He also concluded that while the assailant would look normal enough to avoid notice, there would be some sort of defect that had a negative impact on both his self-esteem and his romantic prospects, something that was entirely outside of his control, but which nonetheless had been a defining factor in his life. Most likely something relatively minor that the perpetrator had blown entirely out of perspective, like a lisp or a stutter. In addition, the profile contained suppositions that anyone could have come to from the case files, but which nonetheless helped to shape the State Trooper's investigation. In particular, the idea that the perpetrator most likely used a plane to get around to the more isolated areas where he killed.

With the combination of this profile and Cindy Paulson's testimony, which had been flagged for their interest due to the accused owning a plane, the state police were able to secure a warrant from a judge to search Robert Hansen's plane, home, and vehicles on October 27th, 1983.

His plane contained no evidence whatsoever of any wrongdoing, although his flight records did match up to the dates when it was supposed that several of the more distant bodies had been calculated to have been left behind. His car had also been cleaned out, and Cindy's shoes, which would have been damning if discovered, were nowhere to be found. One might have assumed that he had been forewarned about the impending searches given just how devoid of evidence the vehicles were, but Robert was habitually cleaning and tidying up as he went about his business. He was organised to an almost pathological degree which is what made him so excellent in the bakery but so difficult to live with otherwise.

The intensive search of his home turned up some much more interesting evidence. The basement had the pillar that Paulson's testimony described, along with the chains, though an argument could be made that these were relatively normal things to find in a basement.

What could not be discounted as normal was the fact that he had created several hiding places in the home where items related to his crimes could be secured and hidden from his family.

In a corner of the attic space, tucked away behind beams and hidden from sight in the main area where his wife and children might venture was a cache of firearms including a number of pistols and the .223 Caliber Ruger Mini-14 semi-automatic rifle that he had used to kill several of his victims. Ballistics testing could not conclusively prove that it was the exact weapon used due to the amount of time that the discarded casings had been exposed to the harsh elements, but it was certainly the same type of weapon used to commit the crimes, and not a very common one.

But amidst all the ammunition boxes stacked neatly away, there was another box, one containing not bullets but jewellery.

The trophies that Robert had been taking from his victims were all there collected in one place. There was a veritable trove of treasures, so many that the wheat and the chaff were essentially impossible to separate. They knew that there were three dead women, and they knew that they needed to find an item of jewellery for each one, but the sheer amount crammed into that little box made their lives difficult. If every item of jewellery that had been taken as a trophy represented a different woman, then this box amounted to a far more widespread massacre than anyone might have guessed. Still, after sifting through it all down at the station, witnesses who knew the victims that had already been discovered were able to identify key items that tied Robert to the crimes.

The police had Robert in custody as a result of the raid on his house, and they had already been presenting such evidence to him as they thought they had in an effort to extract a confession, but he was denying everything. Piece by piece, in little plastic bags, the jewellery was brought in. Photographs of the victims wearing the same jewellery were produced when they could be and signed affidavits from friends and family of the victims when pictures were not available. There was a clear connection between Robert and the dead women. He had a criminal history that involved brutalising prostitutes, and he had the plane that would have been required to ship the women out into the wilderness. Not to mention his incredible hunting skills. Everything pointed towards him being the perpetrator. Yet despite all of it, he denied and denied and denied.

But the search of the house was not yet over. Even as Robert was held in an interrogation cell, the rest of the police were still tearing his home apart. His family was shuttled from room to room, sobbing, as their picturesque little slice of suburbia turned into a crime scene before their eyes. As more and more little pieces of circumstantial evidence were stitched together.

Darla could not believe that Robert was responsible for any of the crimes for which he was accused. He wasn't capable of murder. He went to church with her every Sunday, he said his prayers – a man of the faith could never break its most sacred commandments. She tried to plead with the police not to search the bedroom that she and her husband shared, to leave them that one tiny scrap of privacy and decency. If there had been anything out of order in the room that she slept in, surely, she herself would have seen it, and she had seen nothing.

It was apparent to everyone involved that Darla had no involvement in her husband's crimes and was as surprised as anybody in Anchorage over the accusations levelled at him. But that did not mean that they could trust her word. She had a vested interest in keeping Robert out of jail, even if he was a murderer. So, they began tearing the room apart, going first through all of Robert's drawers, searching for further evidence of his guilt, bloodstains on his clothes, hidden trinkets or papers that might tie together the timelines that they were constructing to track his movements. Next, they moved on to poor Darla's belongings, raking through her underwear and leaving it scattered across the room as she wept by the door. Even flipping the mattress turned up nothing. Whatever hope they had of finding something conclusive enough to break Robert in the interrogation chamber was rapidly slipping away. This was the last room of the house that they had to search. The basement had been bleached clean of any evidence to support their surviving victim's testimony, and while the trove in the attic was sufficient to convince them of his guilt, it may not have been enough to convince a jury of his peers.

Frustrated, one of the cops turned too quickly and stubbed his toe on the bedframe. From behind the headboard, there came a thump. All the cops looked to one another, then converged, pulling the bed away from the wall and revealing an aeronautical map that Robert had inexplicably stowed away behind the headboard of his marital bed. Rolling their eyes, most of the cops returned to work, but one opened the map and studied it.

It was an entirely standard aeronautical map; of the kind any pilot might keep in their plane. The only distinctive thing about this one was the little crosses that had been dotted across it. Scribbled on in pen by Robert. It took only a moment for the officer to make the connection and run to the detective in charge with the map. The victims that they had found all coincided with one of the crosses on the map. The crosses represented locations where Robert had dumped the bodies of his victims.

When the interrogator in the room with Robert paused to step outside and collect another little baggie of evidence, there was no change in the man's demeanour. He had been declaring his innocence for the duration of the interrogation, without any change in tone or cadence. He had done nothing wrong, they had no evidence of any wrongdoing, otherwise, he would have been charged. He had an alibi for the attempted kidnapping that the police were trying to use to tie the whole thing up in a pretty little ribbon for the State's Prosecutor. He could not have done the things that they were claiming that he had done. He could not have killed anyone. He just wasn't that kind of guy. Sure, he'd made mistakes and had some run-ins with the law in his time, but who among them hadn't made a mistake in their life?

But when the map was laid out in front of him, his most well-kept secret, set staring back at him from atop the table, he knew that it was over. Even if he said nothing, they could go out to the locations on that map, find the bodies, lock him up and throw away the key. There was no way that he could pretend that he was anything other than guilty once they started looking at the other sites.

He took a deep breath to steady himself, and then he spoke without stuttering. Those bitches had it coming. Every one of them deserved it. They were whores. Leeches on society. A disease. He had done the cops a favour by getting rid of them. This one had tried to claw out his eyes when he took what he'd paid for. This one had taken off running with his money. What was he meant to do? Let them maul him and rob him? If they'd been good girls, they never would have been in that situation to start with. They were criminals. Evil, fallen women. When he shot one of them, he was doing the world a greater service than all the food that he could put on all the tables around town with his usual hunting. He had done nothing wrong. He was just like them. Just one of the guys. It was the women. They were the problem. They were the liars. The cheats. The thieves. The whores. He was just a normal guy. He was just trying to keep a roof over his head most of the time. Was it so terrible that he needed to blow off steam once in a while? It wasn't his fault that they wouldn't just take his money and do what they were meant to. He didn't force them to be bitches. He just dealt out the consequences for their being bitches.

The transformation that had overtaken Robert shocked the police, most of whom knew him socially from hunting clubs or from visiting his bakery. He had always been so quiet, so nervous, they had never had the faintest suspicion that he could contain such hatred and rage towards women. That is not to say that there weren't some among the local police's numbers who agreed with him, just that they never would have suspected it of Robert, who they had all thought to be thoroughly harmless and utterly henpecked by his wife.

Now that he had begun making excuses for his actions, they were able to secure confessions to those actions, recorded on audiotape to be replayed in court as often as was required to secure his prosecution. But of course, now that they had him for the three crimes for which they suspected him, they had to move on to the far more daunting task of securing his confessions for each of the other little crosses on his map. They had to track down the women from their missing persons reports that he had killed and notify the families to let them know what had happened to their girls. For some families and friends, it would come as a relief to finally know what had happened to their long-missing women, but to others, it would come as a terrible shock that the person that they fully believed was still out in the world somewhere having another adventure was buried in the frozen earth of Alaska.

As each item of jewellery was presented to him, he would make his confession. His confessions accounted for a spree of sexual assaults stretching all the way back to 1971 when Robert and his family first arrived in Alaska. Yet even now when confronted with all the evidence, and with the metaphorical floodgates opened, Robert was still evasive. He would talk quite readily about raping and assaulting unnamed women, but he only confessed to four actual murders. The three bodies that the police already knew about, and one that he expected them to find on the basis of the map. Sherry Morrow, Joanna Messina, Paula Goulding, and the Jane Doe that locals had taken to calling Eklutna Annie. Even he could not provide any useful information that might help to identify her, pointing the police in an entirely incorrect direction when he tried to guess at the girl's origins. Beyond that, he was charged with the kidnap and rape of Cindy Paulson, who had been brought in to positively identify her attacker now that the police felt that there was sufficient evidence to outweigh her own inscrutable nature when it came time for court. Her shoes, abandoned in his car, were never recovered. He had disposed of them somewhere out in the wilderness, just like he'd dumped the property of so many of his victims.

As interviews with Hansen continued over the course of the ongoing police investigations, one other crime was added to the docket. While searching his backyard for any signs of evidence, the police had come across what they suspected to be a burial mound but which was soon proven to be a heap of Robert's trophies. The very ones that he had reported 'stolen' some time ago to commit insurance fraud. The insurance company wasn't going to let something like that slide just because their customer happened to be a mass murderer too. So, an insurance fraud charge was added to the list that Robert was going to be taken to court to answer for.

Andrea Altiery's distinctive fish necklace was found amongst the trophies that Robert genuinely did seem to care about. Without a body ever being discovered, however, it was impossible for the police to charge Robert with Andrea's murder, even though all of her friends were baying for Robert's blood and were entirely certain of his guilt in the matter.

While there are many other murders attributed to Robert Hansen in this book, it is important to note that those six crimes are the only ones that we can be entirely certain were his handiwork. It is possible that there was another serial killer at work in the great state of Alaska at that time who happened to perfectly replicate the way that Robert hunted his prey and chose victims identical to the ones that Robert would have chosen. It is also possible that all the other women who were later discovered died at around the same time but as the result of completely unrelated murders. Possible, but so unlikely as to severely test the limits of credibility.

In the run-up to the trial, the media inevitably went into a frenzy. Serial killers were now a known phenomenon and the specific details of Robert's methodology had been leaked to the press at some point, so the fact that he hunted women for sport had now become public knowledge. For obvious reasons, this meant that it was going to be extraordinarily difficult to offer him a trial by an unbiased jury of his peers.

As such, it came as an immense relief to prosecutors when he announced that he was willing to take a plea deal. He would plead guilty to the four murders that they already had him on and help them decipher his aeronautical map to discover other bodies, so long as he was not charged with any further crimes. In addition, he would be placed into a federal prison after conviction, and there would be no press involvement in any of the proceedings. Ironically, after a lifetime of feeling ignored and overlooked, he now found that he did not want the attention.

The reason for this sudden change of direction was simple. Ballistics reports had finally come back from the victims that had been found that could conclusively connect Robert's rifle with the victims. Where before there could have been some possibility of reasonable doubt, now there was none. All that the prosecution would need to do to win their case would be to convince a jury that the scientific evidence presented was real, and in the 80s, getting people to deny science was a more difficult prospect. With the ballistic evidence, Robert's hopes of escaping consequences for his crimes, as he had for so long, dwindled to nothing. For this reason, he instructed his lawyer to accept the previously offered deal before the newly acquired damning evidence shifted the goalpost further away from his best interests.

Seventeen separate graves were uncovered in the following weeks. Twelve of them were entirely unknown to the investigation before Robert guided the police to them. There were still multiple marks on the map that Robert claimed did not correlate to any murder he was known to have committed, including several around Resurrection Bay. He denied any knowledge of the additional graves and murders that are now commonly believed to include Mary Thill and Megan Emerick. There were, in fact, a great many markings on the map that he told investigators had nothing to do with any illicit activity, they were simply places where he'd sighted a good spot to touch down with his plane, or where he'd spotted deer migrations from the air. It was certainly true that the various markings were not the simple 'x marks the spot' of his burial sites, but that did not mean that there was no correlation between them and all of the many missing women in Alaska who could still not be accounted for.

As a result of this plea deal, Robert felt like there was no longer any danger in discussing his crimes, so it was now possible for the police to actually get some answers out of him. He confirmed their theory about how he was abducting women, using the cunning ploy of offering them money to spend time with him, but provided an additional shocking detail. There were a great many prostitutes beyond the ones that he had killed who he had simply released after his lusts had been slaked. Killing was reserved only for the women that he believed would report his activities to the police, or who had behaved in too defiant a manner during their long sessions of rape and sodomy. This statement was not consistent with the witness testimony of Cindy Paulson, who had been entirely obedient and submissive towards him throughout her abduction. He claimed that he judged her not only on her actions during the event but in the time surrounding it. He admitted to observing his potential victims ahead of time which allowed him to plan ahead for those victims that he knew he would have to dispose of. He often made his decision about whether or not they would be "good girls" before ever making any actual contact.

As a result of the inconsistency between his testimony and that of Paulson, it was suspected that the number of women that he had killed might very well have been considerably higher. All of the prostitutes that he freely admitted to picking up but claimed to have set free might very well have been other victims. While zealous attempts were made to garner more information about these women throughout the numerous interrogations all the way up to trial, there were pitifully few identifying details in Robert's stories that would definitively allow their survival to be confirmed. For this reason, the precise number of women that Robert Hansen killed since his spree began in the 1970s is and shall remain, unknown. At the time, the police settled on a median number of 37 probable victims based on the evidence and testimony that they had managed to secure.

When his day in court came, it was not the moment that any of the families of his victims had been hoping for. There was no sense of relief that their daughter's killer was being punished because even now, everything was happening according to his design. The press was barred from the courtroom, an arrangement had been quietly made behind closed doors. When he received his sentence of four hundred and sixty-one years without any possibility of parole, they should have been granted some sense of victory, but there was none. Robert Hansen wouldn't be able to hurt any more women, but there were so many dead, and so many more families out there knowing exactly the same pain, who would never get any sense of closure, just because Robert had decided not to share any further details of his murders.

The End

In Lewisburg, Pennsylvania, there was a Federal Prison in which Robert Hansen would be confined until 1988, when construction was completed on the Lemon Creek Correctional Center in Juneau, returning him to Alaska. From a brief stay there, he was eventually moved to Spring Creek Correctional Center in Seward, just a little south of Anchorage. The exact reason for Robert's relocations were not clear, though it is possible that the intention was to place him near to his family so that they could more easily visit him.

For many years, Darla and the kids continued to live in Anchorage. She was the breadwinner for the family, so their financial situation wasn't really impacted. Her husband had been living an almost entirely independent life, using his own funds exclusively for his own entertainment and contributing nothing, so on the financial side of things, she wasn't really missing out on much. But of course, her reputation and that of the children were in tatters. She had stood by her husband throughout the trial instead of disavowing him, and for many, in particular the friends and family of Robert's victims, this meant that she was just as bad as him.

She had known all along that something untoward was going on with 'Bob.' They had been through the same thing multiple times through the years, where everything would be quiet for a while, and then she'd hear through the grapevine that he'd been spotted hanging around with one or another prostitute. It was humiliating to her, but in a way, it wasn't so bad. She felt some guilt over the whole thing, as if she should somehow have satiated him better and ensured that he wouldn't have strayed; she was well and truly indoctrinated into the old conservative Christian ideas of a wife as the caregiver for husband and family to the complete exception of her own needs. But she had never guessed that Bob's actions went beyond simply sleeping with these women in the early hours before opening the bakery for the day's business.

She could forgive him for his trespasses. She felt like it was her responsibility, to keep the family together, and to try and steer him towards a more virtuous path. She had submitted to him in all things, accepting all the verbal abuse that he doled out to her and the kids so long as he never raised a hand to any of them. That was another sticking point for her in coming to terms with the fact that her husband could possibly have done the terrible, violent things that he was accused of. He had never hit her, never hurt the kids, despite having all the provocation that would have made a lesser man lash out at them. How could he have had so many opportunities to do them harm, and refused every time, if he was so capable of such horrifying violence? Throughout their whole marriage, she had known that Bob was trouble, but she had always hoped that she was a guiding influence, leading him away from the dark towards the light of the Good Word. At her insistence, Bob attended church with the whole family, even though he much preferred the quiet contemplation of the Alaskan woodlands to any building, even the house of the Lord.

They had stayed together throughout all of his wrongdoing, not only because she believed that she could change him, but also because she believed that it was her duty to submit to her husband, for better or worse. Divorce did not even occur to her as an option, even though they had gradually come to live such entirely separate lives that they may as well not have been together at all.

It would only be after the trial was complete that she finally sought out legal counsel of her own and began divorce proceedings, and even then, it was only because she had learned that there was no possibility of Bob ever getting out of jail in her lifetime. Her values and ideals had made her more vulnerable to Robert's manipulations than anyone, and it is difficult not to think that was a part of what had attracted him to her in the first place. The fact that despite being a well-educated and intelligent woman, she would always have a blind spot when it came to her husband.

Christianity had been a millstone around her neck, keeping her with Robert despite all of the ways that he had wronged her, but in the aftermath of his crimes becoming public, her faith became a rock. The other members of her church knew exactly what Robert had done, but in spite of that, they stood by Darla. All of the neighbours who had lived next to a house where Robert had bound, tortured, and raped women stood by Darla too. In spite of everything that her awful husband had done, she was such a pinnacle of goodness that it was all forgiven and forgotten.

Yet despite this, once the divorce was completed – without any argument or contest from Robert, who firmly believed that she was entitled to the house and any assets – she began to lay out plans to permanently depart from Alaska.

For several years, the location of his family became a carefully guarded secret, as they tried to re-establish their lives. His daughter attended college in Arkansas, where it seems that the family settled for a while. She was an intensely private young woman, who unfortunately seemed to have inherited her father's stutter. Darla continued to teach and care for children. She moved away from caring for the disabled as she grew older and less physically capable of handling students who needed hands-on assistance, instead offering music lessons. When attention once again shone on Robert's case in the 2000s as a result of the increased public interest in true crime, and multiple mass media projects focused on him, including a Nicholas Cage and John Cusack movie called The Frozen Ground, it seems that the family moved on once again. The last unconfirmed reports in 2018 suggest that Darla had actually moved to Russia where she had taken up full-time teaching once more to support herself. Of Robert's son, there has been little trace, and it seems likely that he changed his name and moved away from the family at the earliest opportunity to prevent anyone with prurient interest in the case from pursuing him.

In keeping with Robert's last demand for privacy from the press, he did what he could to draw as little attention to himself as possible. While most other serial killers attempt to appeal their convictions as many times as allowable by the law, Robert simply accepted his lot in life with quiet stoicism. He did not give media interviews, despite almost constant demands for them. In fact, only the Behavioural Analysis Unit of the FBI ever had the opportunity to interview him for their studies. Even that seemed to have been predicated on the personal relationship between John Douglas and Robert, who found the man who had so accurately profiled everything about him to be quite fascinating in his own right.

It was from these interviews that it is possible to discern so many of the discreet psychological details of the crimes, and what drove Robert to commit them. Most important for him was the hunt. When he actually killed a woman, it often came with a sense of anti-climax, it was the end of the fun, after all. But stalking them through the wilderness with a gun or bow, tracking them like animals, pitting himself against an intelligent mind that was trying to outwit him and escape, these were the times that Robert felt most alive. Every other part of the experience was more necessity than joy, he raped the women because he needed a sexual outlet, and an outlet for his anger over a lifetime of being overlooked and rejected, and he killed the women because it was necessary to hide his crimes from the world, but neither of these actions were for the joy of it. They were driven by impulses, both irrational and rational. Only the hunt was his. Only the hunt made him feel good.

Throughout his years of confinement, there would be occasions when Robert might befriend a cellmate or some other prisoner and let slip some details about his crimes that were unknown to the police. These were often dutifully reported with the hope that the one making those reports might receive some favourable treatment in prison. It is from these unsubstantiated reports that it has been possible to construct a larger picture of Robert's murderous spree. Many of the crimes that he committed left behind no physical evidence that has been discovered, and we have only this hearsay to confirm or deny the many allegations levelled against him through the years. Allegations that can never be fully realised but comprise the majority of his crimes and at various times, a great many more relating to missing women in Alaska during that time period.

Due to the gold rush nature of Alaska during the pipeline construction, there were constant, drastic population shifts, and the women that he targeted, generally on the lowest rungs of society, tended to be more itinerant than most. They routinely travelled from town to town and state to state as they followed the easy money, in much the same way that the natives of Alaska had once migrated alongside the deer that they preyed upon. The vast majority of missing persons reports made in Anchorage were never closed, never even followed up on. The city simply didn't have the infrastructure to deal with the massive influx, and subsequent departure, of so many prostitutes, exotic dancers, strippers, and other sex workers. The more popular clubs that offered these services consumed much in terms of police resources as officers often had to be dispatched to them dozens of times in a single night, even during the week when things were meant to be quiet. And along with the influx of prostitutes had come an entourage of other petty criminals. There were pimps, robbers, hucksters, and worse, all preying on the girls and their clients with equal abandon. It was no small wonder, indeed, that there were so many missing women at that time and it was equally understandable how the ones who were legitimately missing had gotten lost in the crossfire and chaos of that period.

It will never be possible to know just how many victims Robert Hansen took out into the woods and stalked for his own sick amusement. Even the fairly comprehensive list of them presented in this book may only represent a fraction of his true inventory of victims. All of the bodies that were recovered were only found because they had been abandoned or had been hurriedly put in a far-too-shallow grave. If there were other bodies laid to rest in the Alaskan wilderness when Robert had not felt particularly harried, in all likelihood they will remain there, entirely undiscovered, for centuries to come. Alternatively, it is entirely possible, although somewhat less likely, that Robert was telling the truth in his interviews with the police, and the seventeen graves he led them to represent the sum of all that he had killed during his decade-long massacre.

He remained hidden from sight, kept a low profile, and allowed the years to wash over him in prison. Looking out across the yard to see the endless snow-covered forests of the national parks that surrounded Spring Creek Correctional Center. His church, his hunting ground, his one true love, all still there, just out of reach.

With age, he began to falter. A lifetime without proper sleep had put immense strain on his body, and slowly but surely the various systems of that body began to fail. In May of 2014, he was transferred to the Anchorage Correctional Complex so that he could receive more medical care than Spring Creek could provide, but even that was insufficient to preserve him any further. He was transferred to Alaska Regional Hospital in

Anchorage in August, finally dying on the 21st of August 2014 at the age of 75. An autopsy determined that this was due to natural causes, and no further investigation was required.

Robert Hansen was dead, and the world could move on.

Except, of course, the world could not move on. There were families that would never be whole again, and far more people out in the world who still didn't have the faintest idea if their friend or loved one had fallen victim to Hansen's murderous rampage. Every woman who had gone missing in Alaska during the period of his active murders could have been a victim, and they numbered in the thousands. Upwards of five thousand women went missing across the years in which he was operating. Any one of them could have been another of his victims, and nobody would ever know. In spite of his occasional slips when talking to other inmates, the full breadth of the crimes that Robert committed will never be known. The only ones who could have told the stories of the dead were the dead, themselves. Even among those known to have been his victims, there are a great many missing bodies. With his car, his plane, and all the time in the world, Robert might well have hidden victims anywhere. It is generally assumed that the aeronautical map that he kept behind his headboard to examine in his private moments was a full catalogue of all the dump sites that he had made use of, but that is purely supposition. There were so many markings on that map that were never deciphered, and there was certainly no guarantee that the one map that was discovered represented the full catalogue of victims. Looking at the trove of trophies that he had taken from women and secreted away with his weapons, only a tiny fraction have been accounted for so far, and we know that he didn't take trophies from all of his victims either, so there might have been even more beyond that. Already a prolific serial killer, Robert Hansen might have been one of the most prolific in American history, without anyone being any the wiser.

Work has continued since his death to identify the remains of the victims that he left behind. More bodies have been discovered and identified, with the timeline of their death and the manner of their killing tying into Robert's hunting trips. Advances in forensic science have allowed genetic testing to be used on some of the bodies, allowing some long overdue identification, giving the dead back their names, and giving their families a small bit of closure. Throughout all of it, Eklutna Annie has remained something of a mystery. Advances in biomedical analysis helped investigators to reach the conclusion that she had likely originated in California as evidenced by the balance of certain proteins and materials found in her system, but with the destruction of her face by scavenging animals, the usual methods that are typically employed to identify a dead person have been left with nothing to work from. Her genetic material has never been successfully matched to any missing person, or even to anyone in any genetic testing system offered commercially or publicly in the USA. She remains a ghost. Buried under the name Jane Doe, with nobody to mourn her, or even to know who she was before Robert Hansen snatched her life away for his own sick amusement.

The National Center for Missing and Exploited Children still has a listing posted for her, providing as full and detailed an account of all that was known about her as it was possible to reconstruct.

The Jane Doe was between 16 and 25 years old. White, with possible Native American ancestry. She was between 4ft 11 inches and 5'1" tall. Her hair was long, light brown with a red tint, and she was found wearing a brown leather jacket, a knit sweater, jeans, red knee-high high-heeled boots, a wide copper bracelet with turquoise stones, a beaded necklace, also with turquoise, gold earrings, a gold ring with a white stone and a gold Timex watch, though this was found separate from the body. In her jacket was a box of Salem matches.

Numerous reconstructions of her face have been made over the years, in a variety of mediums. Pictures have been sketched based on the available information, along with sculpted busts and three-dimensional renderings, all reliant upon cutting-edge forensic science. Yet it has been to no avail.

Even if he lacked the sheer weight of numbers that other serial killers achieved in their lifetimes to make his mark in the history books, there was something about the way that he killed that seemed to resonate with the collective unconscious of mankind. The way that he treated women exactly the same as prey animals are treated showed incredibly clearly how he felt about women.

In 1924, Richard Cornell penned a story that was considered to be outrageous at the time. It was entitled "The Most Dangerous Game." It revolved around a big-game hunter from New York who became shipwrecked on an isolated island and was hunted for sport by a Russian aristocrat who had tired of hunting animals, considering it to be 'unsporting' to pitch human ingenuity against their instincts, and now preferring to try his skills against the titular 'most dangerous game' of mankind. Over the course of the story, the hero outwits his hunter, eventually turning the tables on him and defeating the man at his own game.

It has been called the most popular story ever written in English and received so many adaptations to other media that listing them all would require an entire book in itself.

The story resonated strongly with readers, both in the reversal of roles where a hunter becomes the prey and with those who supported the animal rights movement and saw big-game hunting as tantamount to the atrocity being described in the story. Yet there had been no attempts to recreate such a story in real life before Robert Hansen came along, and there doesn't seem to have been any indication that he had ever even read the story, though it is unlikely he could have escaped all of the film adaptations. While others walked away from such a story thinking that the 'hunter' in each adaptation was mad, Robert came to emulate them instead.

Interestingly, the whole purpose of hunting humans in the story and in most subsequent adaptations was to provide a greater challenge to a highly skilled hunter – a fantasy that likely would have greatly appealed to Robert – the sad truth of the reality, however, was that he did everything in his power short of hobbling the women that he set free to ensure that they could not possibly win the game. Without clothes, in the freezing Arctic winds of Alaska, even if he had not caught up to them in a short time, there was no possibility that any of the women he 'took out to his cabin' were ever going to see another dawn. He picked women from the city who had little to no experience in the wilderness, he stripped them of any protection from the elements, robbed them of any of the tools that they might use to fashion a defence for themselves, and then he set them off running over terrain that he was intimately familiar with, and was considerably skilled in tracking across. There was basically no scenario in which any of the women that he hunted might have escaped. Even if he had somehow failed to track them, the elements or predators would have finished them off long before they got anywhere near civilisation. That was why he took them to such isolated locales.

The goal in the case of Robert Hansen was not to elevate the hunt by introducing a more impressive prey animal but to degrade women into being the equivalent of the deer and sheep that he stalked and killed. Raping them wasn't enough, killing them wasn't enough, he had to turn them into animals. That was how deeply his rage against women went. They had rejected him for being too quiet, for stuttering, for looking disgusting, for not giving him whatever he wanted whenever he wanted it. So, for his revenge, he would make them into beasts, lower than low, and he would do whatever he pleased with them.

The name attached to Robert by the press was the rather uninspired "Butcher Baker" referencing his day-to-day employment as if it was even the slightest factor in his murders. The only reason that he was a baker was because he had been trained to be one and had never found a better option. An argument could be made that the odd work hours contributed to his ability to hunt, but ultimately, he barely slept anyway, so it would have made very little difference. Yet despite attempts by the media to focus on the mundane, it was the fantastical elements of Robert's killing spree that captured the imagination of the public. The fact that he was hunting human beings, not in the savage manner of other serial killers, stalking and breaking into their homes, but in the manner of an actual game hunter. Just as the fictional tale of "The Most Dangerous Game" had been capturing attention for almost a hundred years, now the real-life horrors of Robert Hansen's crimes seemed to replace it in the public consciousness.

The books written by profiler John Douglas helped to plant the seeds for this obsession, with Hansen being the subject of some discussion within them as a result of the Behavioural Analysis Unit's involvement in solving the case. The public's fascination with serial killers and their fascination with Douglas' methods used to track and capture those killers has continued to grow with time, including long-running media spectacles revolving around the Behavioural Analysis Unit's history and fictional versions of it appearing throughout literature and film. The Silence of the Lambs, Criminal Minds, and Mindhunter were all directly inspired by John Douglas' work and as such, representations of many of his past cases have appeared within these series, including fictional versions of Robert Hansen, albeit with various twists on the tale.

With the overwhelming prevalence of police procedural series throughout the 2000s, and the uniqueness of Hansen's crimes, characters representing him have cropped up one or more times in almost all of them. Not to mention the various blends of his true-life story and the Most Dangerous Game that have both appeared unaltered or been twisted for comedic effect in various other media. Even if there had been no influence on fiction as a result of his crimes, the sheer volume of documentaries about the case could fill several weeks' worth of viewing time. Robert might have died, but it seems that his story never will, being repeated endlessly by the fascinated public who are trying desperately to understand what might have driven a man to do the things that he did.

Doctors described him as suffering from 'manic depression' and 'intermittent schizophrenia' but neither of these conditions make a person a killer. Quite the opposite in fact, people with those medical conditions are statistically far more likely to become victims of violence than they ever are to perpetrate it. His massive mood swings were certainly a factor in some of the high-risk behaviour that he undertook, up to and including the frankly deranged actions that led to some of his previous brushes with the law. But fundamentally it was not a mental illness that made Robert into the man he was, but his obsessions. Where other people grow and change, Robert never did. He remained in a state of arrested development from his teenage years on, just as angry when he was an old man in jail as when he was a spotty-faced teenager being turned down by girls. He could never move past the things that had irked him. He constantly thought about every perceived slight he had received in his lifetime, blowing them entirely of proportion.

While many of us can look back at bad things that happened to us and learn from them, moving past them to become better people, Robert could not. There is an argument to be made that the abuse he suffered at the hands of his father, and the levels of stress that he was under as a child may have amplified his perception of everyday problems that affect us all, and made him respond to them as though they were traumatic, but once again, there are a great many people in the world who suffered exactly the same 'trauma' or worse and managed not to murder anyone as a result.

The sad truth of the matter is that Robert was an unhappy child who grew into an unhappy man, and rather than looking inward to recognise the faults in himself that ensured that the endless cycle of misery would continue, he turned his rage out onto the world. He sought out innocent people that he could act out his revenge fantasies on so that he could feel some momentary elation. Ultimately, he wanted revenge on everyone in the world, for the terrible crime of not being as miserable as him.

Women had rejected him as a teenager, because he was socially inept, suffered from a skin condition that made him look unattractive and had basically nothing to offer them except for his overwhelming sense of being entitled to their bodies. Most men represented his father in his mental landscape, cruel and relentless authority figures that he had to outwit, or best, if he wanted to find any pleasure in life. The only person in Robert Hansen's world who was real, was him. This may sound like schizophrenia, but it was in effect an extreme form of narcissism. He had learned from an early age that there was nobody else that he could rely on, and that external forces were almost always universally going to be trying to cause him harm, which meant that despite him having cripplingly low self-esteem, he was nonetheless the only person that truly mattered. Other people caused pain, and only he could create pleasure for himself. With that in mind, it is possible to see how he came to the conclusions that he did and took the actions that he eventually would. Nobody else was real, so he wasn't doing real harm to any of them. There was no benefit to him in helping others find peace over their lost loved ones, so he never offered help. His family, such as it was, existed only as an extension of himself, to serve him better as a signal to others that he was both normal and successful in that area of life. His business, which was the envy of many, existed for the same purpose. Sometimes he needed money to get the things that he wanted, so owning a successful bakery was helpful in that respect, but the business itself brought him no joy; perhaps if he had not been raised in a bakery by his domineering father, things would have been different, but he went through his tasks mechanically, as quickly as possible, so that he could get on to the next thing that he actually wanted to do. Much like he engaged with most of the things in his life.

Hunting seemed to be the only exception from this, the only thing that he truly loved doing for its own sake, but it is difficult in retrospect to view this particular violent hobby to be anything other than a prelude to the actual hunting that he enjoyed the most. It may have provided him with some relief, it may have been that he fantasised about the animal in his sights actually being a person. While other serial killers might have laid in bed at night and concocted their own murderous scenarios for self-gratification, Robert was never in his bed. The only time that he wasn't working at full pelt in his early life was when he was out in the silence of the woods, stalking and killing. It was the only time that his imagination might have found some opportunity to stretch. Small wonder then, that hunting became the pivotal fixation of his entire murderous spree. That the hunt became so ingrained in him as the most vital part of the process, surpassing even the desire to rape or kill. The murders that he found the most satisfaction in were not the ones where the women fought back like people and he was forced to put them down to prevent problems coming his way, but the murders when he got to play out his hunting fantasy to completion. The hunt was the fantasy. The degradation of women to the status of animals was more enjoyable to him than having sex with them, or even killing them. The process was what he enjoyed, not the product.

This hardly made him unique. Most serial killers who are sexual sadists – which is to say, most serial killers – enjoy the act of torturing and killing their victims more than having the resultant body to deal with. Necrophiliacs and cannibals are the exception rather than the rule. Even for those misogynistic killers who want women to feel like they are nothing, the act of killing is usually the highlight of the event, the moment when they take absolutely everything from their victim. For Robert, it wasn't. Hunting the women that he chose as his victims was what brought him the most joy, not killing them. While he was hunting them, they were terrified, alone, certain of their own death, but in his mind, they were stripped of all that, of all higher brain functions entirely. When he hunted women he felt like he had reduced them to nothing but animals, and that was his most treasured experience. Feeling, however briefly, like he was superior. Like he was the one in control. Taking back control from the women who he felt had controlled him throughout his whole life.

The combination of extreme narcissism and sexual sadism drives many serial killers, and those that experience any degree of self-reflection usually come to use this to justify their actions in a sort of utilitarian manner. Killing and torturing brought them more joy than it caused pain to others, so it was morally correct. Yet in Robert Hansen's case, there seems to have been no self-reflection whatsoever. He scarcely even seemed to be aware that he was acting out his fantasies of revenge on the women who had rejected him in his youth. He barely seemed aware of anything. Ironically, even as he tried to strip his victims of all their humanity and leave them as nothing but creatures of instinct at his mercy, he revealed himself to be exactly that. There was no reason or logic to his actions beyond a base animal urge to hunt and kill. To exert dominance and feel like the strongest animal. In essence, by trying to strip the humanity from others, he made himself into a beast.

From the cradle, he had been made into an animal. He was deprived of sleep, browbeaten and yelled at constantly to ensure his compliance. He was incapable of forming normal social bonds and was only ever rewarded for his talent for killing. It should come as no surprise that Robert ended up an outcast with no interest in fitting into civilisation. The wild places of the world were the only ones where he felt truly at home, truly safe, with any danger clearly visible before it struck, unlike the endless hidden dangers lurking just out of sight in civilisation. In the classroom or the dance hall, being unable to speak was a massive impediment to success, but out in the wild places, his silence was the greatest of all possible advantages.

Being dull and motionless, being ugly and beneath notice, these were traits that carried social death sentences in the world he'd been born into, but in the world that he found just outside the streetlights and noise, they were advantageous. When he was on the hunt, he felt powerful in a way that society would never have allowed him to feel. It was unsurprising that he chose that over the promise that obeying the rules and doing the right thing would someday pay off.

And so, like an animal, he sought the things that brought him pleasure, avoided the things that caused him pain, and thought little about either one of them beyond the moment. When he raped and tortured, it felt good, so he didn't care about the horrific harm he was doing to his victims. When he hunted and when he killed, he would no sooner shed a tear for one of the women that he had downed than he would the prize buck whose antlers would be decorating his wall come springtime. Empathy was something that human beings extended to other human beings, and something that it seemed Robert had entirely lost at some point during his upbringing. In a way, this lack of empathy was entirely self-serving. He couldn't feel bad for his victims, so he never had to change his behaviour, abandoning the things that made him feel good, even as they did others harm. Whether he truly felt no hint of remorse, or if he crushed it for fear of it interfering in his joyous hunts, we will never know.

Robert Hansen spent his entire adult life hiding who he was, giving away only enough to provide him with an advantage in any given situation. He formed relationships with others based purely on what those relationships could provide to him and relied upon the fact that his appearance and mannerisms were so thoroughly mundane that he would escape notice in almost any situation. The reason that we do not know how many victims he took in his lifetime is that Robert did not wish for us to know. The reason that one of his victims remains entirely without identity, even after all this time, is because Robert did not want us to know. He needed to have absolute control over all information in his life or he no longer felt safe. Even when his honesty would have helped people, even when his honesty might have helped himself, he chose to keep everything a secret rather than risk the mortifying ordeal of being known by others. Did he do all of this because of the horrific double life that he was leading, murdering women for his own gratification? Because he did not consider other people to be real people thanks to his intense narcissism? Because controlling information was a way for him to retain the feeling of power that he got when he was out hunting? We will never know the answers to any of these questions. We will never know who Eklutna Annie was in life. We will never know how many dead women lie in shallow graves scattered across Alaska, as yet unfound, or how many of the bodies that have been found across the state were thanks to his handiwork. We will never know any of these things, because Robert did not wish for us to know.

Want More?

Did you enjoy *The Hunt* and want some more True Crime?

YOUR FREE BOOK IS WAITING

**From bestselling author
Ryan Green**

There is a man who is officially classed as "**Britain's most dangerous prisoner**"

The man's name is Robert Maudsley, and his crimes earned him the nickname "**Hannibal the Cannibal**"

This free book is an exploration of his story...

 *"Ryan brings the horrifying details to life. I can't wait to read more by this author!"*

Get a free copy of **Robert Maudsley: Hannibal the Cannibal** when you sign up to join my Reader's Group.

www.ryangreenbooks.com/free-book

Every Review Helps

If you enjoyed the book and have a moment to spare, I would really appreciate a short review on Amazon. Your help in spreading the word is gratefully received and reviews make a huge difference to helping new readers find me. Without reviewers, us self-published authors would have a hard time!

Type in your link below to be taken straight to my book review page.

US	geni.us/HuntUS
UK	geni.us/HuntUK
Australia	geni.us/HuntAUS
Canada	geni.us/HuntCAN

Thank you! I can't wait to read your thoughts.

About Ryan Green

Ryan Green is a true crime author who lives in Herefordshire, England with his wife, three children, and two dogs. Outside of writing and spending time with his family, Ryan enjoys walking, reading and windsurfing.

Ryan is fascinated with History, Psychology and True Crime. In 2015, he finally started researching and writing his own work and at the end of the year, he released his first book on Britain's most notorious serial killer, Harold Shipman.

He has since written several books on lesser-known subjects, and taken the unique approach of writing from the killer's perspective. He narrates some of the most chilling scenes you'll encounter in the True Crime genre.

You can sign up to Ryan's newsletter to receive a free book, updates, and the latest releases at:

WWW.RYANGREENBOOKS.COM

More Books by Ryan Green

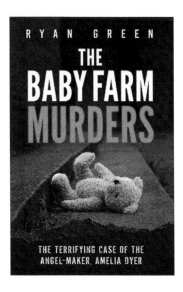

In Victorian England, 1896, Evelina Marmon gave birth to an illegitimate daughter, Doris.

She chanced upon a newspaper advert, could this home be the baby's good fortune?

But Mrs Harding had no intention of caring for Doris. She wasn't married, and her real name was Amelia Dyer. She wanted money.

Amelia never passed on a new address to the anxious mother. Instead, she found some dressmaking tape and bound it tightly around Doris's neck, watching and waiting. She disposed of the body in the river Thames and pawned the clothes Evelina had packed.

The Baby Farm Murders is a chilling account of Amelia Dyer, who was responsible for the deaths of up to 400 children, making her one of the most prolific serial killers in True Crime history. Ryan Green provides a suspenseful narrative that draws the reader into the real-life horror experienced by the victims with all the elements of a captivating thriller.

More Books by Ryan Green

In 1978, Cheryl Bradshaw was a contestant on the popular TV matchmaking show, 'The Dating Game'. From a lineup of eligible bachelors, she selected the handsome daredevil photographer, Rodney Alcala.

As the charmed audience watched the couple embrace, a chilling truth lurked behind the camera lens. Rodney Alcala was a serial killer in the midst of a chilling rampage. Hiding in plain sight.

Alcala lured in his victims by offering them the chance to be a part of his professional photography portfolio, with the promise of launching their modelling careers. But the 1,020 photographs, later found in a secret storage locker by the police, revealed a devastating ulterior motive.

Smile is a chilling account of Rodney Alcala, one of the most prolific serial killers in American history. Ryan Green gives a suspenseful narrative that draws the reader into the real-life horror experienced by the victims with all the elements of a captivating thriller.

More Books by Ryan Green

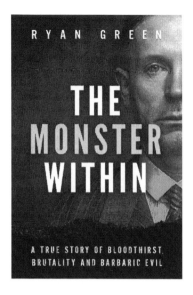

Prostitutes and animals could no longer satisfy Peter Kürten's sexual deviancy. During a burglary of a local tavern, he stumbled upon a nine-year-old girl asleep in her bed. He strangled her, slashed her throat with a pocket knife, and orgasmed upon hearing her blood drip to the floor.

His crimes were halted by World War I and an eight-year prison sentence but he unleashed his urges with a spate of brutal murders in 1929 earning him the nickname "The Düsseldorf Monster".

No one was safe. He committed ferocious attacks, sexual assaults and murder against men, women and children. He used blunt objects, sharp implements or his bare hands, before drinking their blood for sexual satisfaction.

The Monster Within is a chilling account of Peter Kurten, one of the most terrifying serial killers in true crime history. Ryan Green's riveting narrative draws the reader into the real-live horror experienced by the victims and has all the elements of a classic thriller.

More Books by Ryan Green

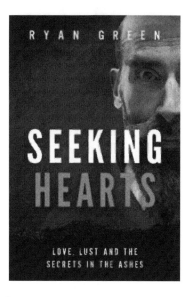

When Inspector Belin set out to catch the elusive Henri Landru for embezzlement and fraud, he wasn't prepared for the complex web of secrets that would unravel.

As war raged on and husbands fought on distant battlefields, Landru preyed upon the vulnerable hearts of lonely young women, presenting himself as a grieving widower desperate to fill the void in his shattered life.

Beneath the façade of a broken man lay a disturbing truth - a predator driven by insatiable desires. Would some of Landru's 283 targets find out in time to save themselves?

Seeking Hearts is a chilling journey through the depths of human darkness. As the riveting tale unfolds, it forces readers to confront the unsettling realisation that, for Henri Landru, murder became the ultimate means of tying up loose ends.

Free True Crime Audiobook

Sign up to Audible and use your free credit to download this collection of twelve books. If you cancel within 30 days, there's no charge!

WWW.RYANGREENBOOKS.COM/FREE-AUDIOBOOK

"Ryan Green has produced another excellent book and belongs at the top with true crime writers such as M. William Phelps, Gregg Olsen and Ann Rule" –**B.S. Reid**

"Wow! Chilling, shocking and totally riveting! I'm not going to sleep well after listening to this but the narration was fantastic. Crazy story but highly recommend for any true crime lover!" –**Mandy**

"Torture Mom by Ryan Green left me pretty speechless. The fact that it's a true story is just...wow" –**JStep**

"Graphic, upsetting, but superbly read and written" –**Ray C**

WWW.RYANGREENBOOKS.COM/FREE-AUDIOBOOK

Printed in Great Britain
by Amazon

52490457R00072